The
Reference Shelf ®

U.S. National Debate Topic 2016–2017

U.S.-China Relations

The Reference Shelf
Volume 88 • Number 3
H.W. Wilson
A Division of EBSCO Information Services

Published by
GREY HOUSE PUBLISHING
Amenia, New York
2016

The Reference Shelf

The books in this series contain reprints of articles, excerpts from books, addresses on current issues, and studies of social trends in the United States and other countries. There are six separately bound numbers in each volume, all of which are usually published in the same calendar year. Numbers one through five are each devoted to a single subject, providing background information and discussion from various points of view and concluding with an index and comprehensive bibliography that lists books, pamphlets, and articles on the subject. The final number of each volume is a collection of recent speeches. Books in the series may be purchased individually or on subscription.

Publisher's Cataloging-In-Publication Data
(Prepared by The Donohue Group, Inc.)

Names: H.W. Wilson Company.
Title: U.S. national debate topic, 2016-2017. U.S.-China relations / [compiled by]
    H. W. Wilson, a division of EBSCO Information Services.
Other Titles: US national debate topic, 2016-2017. U.S.-China Relations | United
    States national debate topic, 2016-2017. U.S.-China Relations | U.S.-China
    Relations | United States-China Relations | Reference shelf ; v. 88, no. 3.
Description: Amenia, New York : Grey House Publishing, 2016. | Includes
    bibliographical references and index.
Identifiers: ISBN 978-1-68217-065-6 (v. 88, no. 3) |
  ISBN 978-1-68217-062-5 (volume set)
Subjects: LCSH: United States--Foreign relations--China. | China--Foreign
    relations--United States. | United States--Foreign economic relations--China. |
    China--Foreign economic relations--United States.
Classification: LCC E183.8.C6 U8 2016 | DDC 327.73051--dc23

Contents

3

Human Rights, Citizen Workers, and Dissidents

4

International Relations and Diplomacy

Preface

China and America: A Troubled Past and Hopeful Future

China maintains one of the oldest written historical records in the world, tracing back the development of Chinese society more than 4,000 years. In the ancient world, Chinese artisans and inventors developed innovations that transformed the world, including papermaking, the first compass that enabled ships to navigate the vast ocean passages, and gunpowder, with its many transformative *and* destructive ramifications. While China is not home to the world's oldest civilization, historians sometimes call China the oldest "continuous society," because ancient Chinese culture was never completely obliterated by war or cultural upheaval, and elements of ancient Chinese culture and tradition survived from antiquity to today.

By comparison, the United States is a young nation that has nonetheless transformed into one of the most influential nations in the world. Though Chinese society had already endured invasions, nationwide wars, and a multitude of other transformative events by the time the United States first formed, by the dawn of the 2010s, China and the United States were the world's two most powerful economies. As two of the most the most influential nations in the world, China and the United States have taken new steps to deepen cooperation and to form trade and diplomatic agreements meant to foster a lasting peace between the two nations. However, the ideological divide between Chinese and U.S. culture, and the uncertainty of future U.S. and Chinese political transformation leaves the future of U.S.-China relations uncertain.

History of U.S.-China Relations

The first U.S. diplomatic contact with China occurred in 1784, when the U.S. ship, the *Empress of China* arrived in Guangzhou, China, marking the beginning of U.S. trade in tea, silk, and spices. The first Chinese laborers began arriving in the United States in the 1840s and 1850s. Historical records indicate that more than 100,000 Chinese laborers arrived in the United States during the first 20 years of open immigration and the influx of Chinese labor was essential to the construction of the U.S. railroad system and the California Gold Rush. Racism and prejudice led to political concerns about the number of new arrivals from China and Congress began placing restrictions on Chinese immigration in the 1870s, culminating in the 1882 Chinese Exclusion Act banning all future immigration from China. The controversial legislation led to nearly 60 years of restricted contact and strained relations between the two nations. Violence against Chinese laborers occurred in some U.S. communities, while in China citizens organized boycotts against American trade in the early 1900s in protest over immigration restrictions.[1]

The United States and China were allies in World War I, and the United States supported the efforts of the Chinese Nationalist Party to unify the nation under a republican government. During World War II, as Japanese forces attempted to capture vast portions of China, the United States extended credit and supplies to the Nationalist regime. In 1942, China and the United States forged an official military alliance, and the following year the United States began allowing the immigration of a small number of Chinese immigrants each year. After World War II, the United States briefly tried to intervene, as an arbiter, in the civil war between Chinese Nationalists and the Chinese Communist Party. When the Communist Party won the civil war, establishing the People's Republic of China in 1949, the United States was in the grips of a period of fervent anti-communist sentiment. China and the former Soviet Union became allies shortly after the formation of the People's Republic of China's official government. As many in the United States considered the Soviet Union to be the nation's chief enemy in the postwar world, China's ties to the Soviets deepened distrust between China and the United States.[2]

During the Cold War, the United States used political and economic influence in an effort to weaken China's communist government and destabilize the nation's position in the international community. The United States formed alliances with the Nationalist remnant government in Taiwan, which fled after the Communist Party took over mainland China. During the Korean War, Chinese and U.S. forces clashed along the border of China. In the 1960s though, Chinese-U.S. relations improved somewhat with the end of U.S. sanctions against Chinese immigration. However, both nations became embroiled in indirect conflict as Communists supported North Vietnam, while the United States supported South Vietnam during the Vietnam War.

As China's relationship with the Soviet Union began to deteriorate, the United States made overtures towards the normalization of diplomatic relations. President Richard Nixon visited China in 1972, providing a symbolic shift in the relationship between the two nations. Though still politically opposed and wary of each other's military capabilities, China-U.S. relations strengthened through trade agreements in the 1970s and 1980s. From 1980 to the 2000s, the economic relationship between the two nations has improved steadily in terms of trade and economic cooperation, though tensions remain over issues such as military de-escalation, territorial expansion, and human rights.

Key Issues in U.S.-China Relations

In the wake of the Cold War, the relationship between the United States and China improved largely due to trade. The liberalization of trade benefitted both nations, but also raised concerns about increasing financial interdependence. Since the 1990s, U.S. economists and politicians have raised concerns about the United States' dependence on China in dealing with the national debt and U.S. dependence on Chinese manufacturing. Similarly, China has long depended on U.S. trade and consumers to purchase the nation's manufactured goods, and on American corporations outsourcing manufacturing to China. In 2016, the United States and China were the world's two largest economies. The Chinese population, for instance, accounts for more than 40 percent of the global coal market, and purchases more rare minerals than the whole of the European Union each year. The United States has similar global influence in terms of both manufacturing and the purchase of manufactured products and natural resources.[3] In the 2010s, China has taken a more active role in the international financial community, expanding aid and development investment in Africa and across Asia. China has also taken steps towards expanding its role as a donor to the international development banks that fund infrastructure and community development programs.[4]

Human rights remain one of the key tensions between the United States and China in the 2010s. While both China and the United States have made significant progress in addressing their respective human rights issues, U.S. politicians and the press openly criticize China for maintaining a repressive regime, while China alleges separate criticisms of the U.S. human rights record as well. While some believe that the U.S. government should strongly pressure the Chinese government to relax social controls and authoritarian governmental policies, the U.S. government has so far criticized China's approach to governance, civil rights, and human rights, while continuing to deepen the U.S.-China economic relationship. The United States is not the only major trading partner to criticize China for human rights violations. Moving forward, it remains to be seen whether China will be able to satisfactorily address the nation's ongoing human rights issues to pave the way for better social/diplomatic relationships in the international community.[5]

China and the United States have also clashed over territorial issues, especially with regard to Chinese expansion into the South China Sea. The tense conflict surrounding China's oceanic territorial expansion also tests U.S. policy with regard to the Philippines and Vietnam, two of the nations that have felt threatened by China's militarization of the sea. U.S. opposition to China's South China Sea operations has been measured, but China's continued development in the region threatens global free trade and has led to a debate about United Nations protocols regarding the ownership of oceanic territory. A number of United States human rights organizations and politicians have also criticized China's ongoing occupation of Tibet and Chinese policies towards the disputed territory of Taiwan. In both cases, China's foreign expansion or control of disputed territories has been a source of tension between China and the United States for decades.

Finally, the United States and China are two of the world's most ecologically destructive nations, both because of sheer population size, and because both nations consume vast amounts of fossil fuels and consume vast amounts of natural resources. As such, both China and the United States have promised to increase their focus on green and sustainable energy and to reduce carbon consumption in the coming decades. While China's environmental crisis is more severe, with air and water pollution in mainland China reaching epidemic proportions, the United States too is facing an environmental and resource crisis without significant reform. The United States and China took the first steps towards the formation of environmental partnerships in the 2010s, potentially paving the way for innovative cooperative ventures in alternative technology in the future.[6]

An Uncertain Future

Since the turbulent Cold War, the United States and China have made strides to-wards the formation of a mutually beneficial, occasionally cooperative relationship. China's rapid growth to become the world's second largest economy in the 1990s, has thrust the nation onto the world stage after decades of relative isolation. China is one of the only nations in the world that could soon rival the United States in terms of military investment, global influence, and economic power. For these reasons, many U.S. politicians and foreign policy specialists believe it is essential that the United States must remain committed to developing deeper, cooperative relations with China. Despite wide-ranging ideological differences and frequent criticism of each other's foreign policy, the increasing economic ties between the two nations have benefitted both. Future avenues of cooperation could lead to major changes in global economics and potentially towards new environmental legislation and reform that could reduce the pace of the planet's growing ecological crisis.

Though there are many substantive issues, from basic philosophical differences to deeply competitive policies separating the United States and China, both nations have made strides to combat the prejudice and bias that developed between the two populations during the long ideological conflict of the Cold War. American opinions of China and Chinese opinions of American culture, however, continue to be influenced by ancient biases and prejudices. As two of the world's most influential societies, peaceful cooperation between China and the United States is not only in the interest of the Chinese and American people, but also serves global interests, helping to prevent violence and conflict between global superpowers so that the resources of the world's largest economies can focus on innovation and development that will benefit the global population.

Micah L. Issitt

Recommended Readings

"Chronology of U.S.-China Relations, 1784–2000." *State*. U.S. Department of State. Office of the Historian. 2000. Web. 26 Apr 2016.

"Country Reports on Human Rights Practices for 2015." *State*. Bureau of Democracy, Human Rights and Labor. U.S. Department of State. 2015. Web. 26 Apr 2016.

"The Indispensable Economy?" *The Economist*. The Economist Newspaper Limited. Oct 28 2010. Web. 25 Apr 2016.

Taylor, Lenore. "US and China Strike Deal on Carbon Cuts in Push for Global Climate Change Pact." *The Guardian*. Guardian News and Media. Nov 12 2014. Web. 26 Apr 2016.

"U.S.-China Relations Since 1949." *Columbia University*. Columbia University. Asia for Educators. 2009. Web. 25 Apr 2016.

Yun, Sun. "China's Foreign Aid Reform and Implications for Africa." *Brookings*. Brooking Institution. Africa in Focus. Jul 1 2015. Web. 25 Apr 2016.

Notes

1. "Chronology of U.S.-China Relations, 1784–2000," *U.S. Department of State.*
2. "U.S.-China Relations Since 1949," *Columbia University.*
3. "The Indispensable Economy?" *The Economist.*
4. Yun, "China's Foreign Aid Reform and Implications for Africa."
5. "Country Reports on Human Rights Practices for 2015," *State.*
6. Taylor, "US and China Strike Deal on Carbon Cuts in Push for Global Climate Change Pact."

1
Economic Growth, Challenges, and Competition

ChinaFotoPress/Getty Images News

Investors observe the stock market at an exchange hall on January 6, 2016 in Beijing, China.

The Era of Economic Giants

For nearly 2000 years, China has maintained one of the world's largest economies. With a population of 1.3 billion in 2013, constituting 18.72 percent of the entire global population, China's hunger for international products drives the global economy. China also has had one of the world's fastest growing economies since the late 1970s, with an average of 10 percent growth per year from 1978 to 2014. In general, measuring economic power involves measuring Gross Domestic Product (GDP), which provides a broad estimate of a nation's economic activity and of the monetary goods produced within a nation.[1] As of 2016, the United States had the world's largest GDP, at an estimated $19 trillion, while China had the world's second largest GDP at $12 trillion. By comparison, Japan has the world's third largest GDP, with an estimated value of $4.3 trillion.[2] While the United States is generally recognized as the world's economic leader, China outpaces the United States in Purchasing Power Parity (PPP), which is a measure of the rate at which the currency of one nation needs to be converted to the currency of another nation to purchase the same amount of goods and services. By any measure, the United States and China are the world's most powerful economies and their purchasing power and trade has a dramatic effect on global economics.

The size of a nation's economy provides a way to estimate the nation's export and purchasing power, but does not provide a reliable estimate about quality of life, or the specifics of how a nation's economic benefits are distributed. Despite its economic power, China is a developing economy with a per-capita (income per person in the population) income well below that of many other advanced nations. With high poverty rates, a potential future real estate crisis, and severe environmental problems, China faces drastic economic challenges moving forward. The Chinese government's new Five-Year Plan (begun in 2016) seeks to address some of the nation's current economic challenges, with strategies to combat poverty, enact governmental financial reform, and shift the nation towards renewable and green energy.

China's Economic Influence

With a large population and unparalleled levels of industrial manufacturing, China's imports and exports have an enormous impact on the global economy. China has been the world's leading exporter since 2009, with an estimated $4 trillion in trade in 2014 alone.[3] China has Free Trade Agreements with several nations, including Australia, South Korea, and the ASEAN alliance. Free Trade Agreements lower the cost of trade between nations, including a reduction on trade tariffs and quotas that may otherwise discourage economic partnerships. In 2015, China surpassed Canada as the United States' largest trading partner, with $441.6 billion in trade recorded between the two nations. In the 2010s, China also became the biggest trading partner in the continent of Africa, with an estimated $166 billion in 2014, which is expected to increase to $1.7 trillion by 2030.[4] China's extensive trade networks fuel the international economy and numerous smaller nations are highly dependent on both Chinese products and on the Chinese demand for exports. For instance, trade from China constitutes more than 10 percent of the GDP for Chile and Indonesia, and China purchases more than 18 percent of Brazil's annual exports.[5]

In 2015 and 2016, China's economy weakened, with reduced growth and stock fluctuations sparking concern around the world of a pending Chinese recession. The 2016 fluctuations in China's economy resulted in reduced profits for hundreds of international corporations, including car companies like BMW and Volkswagen, fashion clothiers like Prada and Coach, and tech companies like Apple and Microsoft. In the wake of China's stock fluctuations, numerous newspapers and magazines speculated about the potential consequences of a recession in China for the rest of the world. In a 2015 article for *CNN*, Patrick Gillespie explained that a reduction in Chinese agricultural imports like sugar, coffee, and soybeans, affects agricultural producers in South America (like Chile and Brazil), thus reducing the demand for agricultural products like riding tractors, pesticides, and other equipment manufactured in other nations. As a result, a reduction in Chinese agricultural imports can have a ripple effect that ultimately impacts U.S. companies like John Deere, which sells riding tractors and agricultural equipment in the South American market.[6]

Economic Partnerships

Economic cooperation and trade agreements have been the keys to the developing peace between the United States and China since the end of the Cold War. The opening of trade between the two nations in the 1970s provided both nations with a way to end the economic stagnation that had gripped both nations during the 1960s. Over the decades, U.S.-China trade increased, becoming an essential feature of both economies. Though China's wide-reaching trade agreements protected the nation from the U.S. recession of 2008 and 2009, China is dependent on U.S. trade to maintain growth. Similarly, the United States depends on inexpensive Chinese manufacturing and labor. The Chinese market also absorbs a significant amount of U.S. debt. As of 2015, China controlled some $1.22 trillion in U.S. debt (8 percent) in the form of treasury bills and bonds.[7]

Given the links between the Chinese and U.S. economies, maintaining the nation's economic partnerships has been a priority for U.S. and Chinese governmental administrations since the 1980s. At a series of meetings held between 2013 and 2015, Presidents Barack Obama and Xi Jinping of China established a set of joint goals for furthering economic cooperation between the two nations. Press releases from the meetings highlighted both nations' commitments to multilateral development banks (MDBs), which are international financing organizations set up and funded by international investment that serve to provide financing in developing nations. Both President Obama and President Xi pledged to increase their nations' respective investment in MDBs and to increase development in the World Bank and other global or regional banking institutions that fund development projects abroad. Economists frequently complain that China is too secretive regarding the nation's financial situation, which discourages foreign investment. At the meetings between Xi and Obama, President Xi also pledged to work with the International Monetary Fund (IMF) to enhance transparency in an effort to increase foreign investment and economic cooperation.[8] President Xi's pledges for future economic cooperation come as China, in general, has been increasing involvement in international financial partnerships. China led the effort to establish the Asian Infrastructure Investment Bank, a 57-nation investment organization meant to foster financial integration and cooperation in the region. China also invested heavily in the "One Belt, One Road" initiative designed to build new ports and energy facilities across Eurasia and East Africa.

China's Economic Future

Since 1953, the Chinese government has organized its financial initiatives within the framework of "five-year plans" in which the government seeks to reach certain economic goals. Each of China's five-year plans since the 1960s has included alleviating poverty as one of the nation's chief goals, though poverty remains a major problem for millions in China. Since the 1980s, China's economic strategies have reduced the poverty rate from 49 percent in 1981 to 6.5 percent in 2012. Estimates from the World Bank indicate that China's poverty rate continued to fall, reaching an estimated 4.1 percent in 2014.[9]

China's 12th Five Year Plan (2011–2016) included plans for new hydropower facilities to reduce the nation's dependence on fossil fuels and also saw the construction of 36 million low income apartment facilities in China's cities in an effort to address poverty and income inequality. China's severe pollution issues have made environmental reform a major part of all governmental economic and development plans in the 2010s. One of the cornerstones of China's 13th Five Year Plan, which began in 2016, was to promote and increase investment in green energy across the nation. China has also entered into a partnership with the World Bank, known as the China 2030 initiative, to expand healthcare and educational programs for low income residents across China. These programs, in concert with broader plans to increase investment in multinational banking and to invest in economic development in Africa and other developing nations, are intended to provide for China's economic future, opening new markets to fuel the nation's growth.[10]

Evidence of an economic downturn in early 2016 inspired widespread speculation that China's governmental debt could lead to a serious collapse akin the 2008–2009 U.S. recession. Writing in *The Wall Street Journal*, James Zimmerman argued that the Chinese government's failure to enact serious financial reforms was one of the reasons that the nation was facing a potential financial crisis. Though China has taken steps to engage more fully in the global economy, China's complicated trade laws complicate this process. Numerous international corporations hoping to eventually conduct business in China have been waiting, for instance, for China to enact trade reforms promised at the beginning of the 12th Five Year

Plan in 2011.[11] Despite the possibility of a financial crisis and numerous economic challenges, China remains one of the world's most economically powerful nations and one of the United States' most valuable economic partners. Moving forward, both nations must continue looking for ways to work together while addressing the difficult challenges of environmental restoration and working together to aid in the growth of developing nations.

Micah L. Issitt

Recommended Readings

Callen, Tim. "Gross Domestic Product: An Economy's All." *IMF*. International Monetary Fund. Mar 28 2012. Web. 20 Apr 2016.

"China 2030: Building a Modern, Harmonious, and Creative Society." *World Bank*. International Bank for Reconstruction and Development. 2013. Web. 20 Apr 2016.

"China Economic Growth Slowest in 25 Years." *BBC News*. Jan 19 2016. Web. 20 Apr 2016.

"China's 8-7 National Poverty Reduction Program." *Worldbank*. The World Bank. Shanghai Poverty Conference. 2004. Web. 26 Apr 2016.

Esposito, Mark and Terence Tse. "China Is Expanding Its Economic Influence in Africa. What Is Africa Getting Out of It?" *Slate*. Slate Group. Nov 24 2015. Web. 20 Apr 2016.

"FACT SHEET: U.S.-China Economic Relations." *Whitehouse*. Office of the Press Secretary. Sep 25 2015. Web. 20 Apr 2016.

Gillespie, Patrick. "China Contagion: How it Ripples Around the World." *CNN Money*. Cable News Network. Aug 26 2015. Web. 20 Apr 2016.

Monaghan, Angela. "China Surpasses US as World's Largest Trading Nation." *The Guardian*. Guardian News and Media. Jan 10 2014. Web. 20 Apr 2016.

Rapoza, Kenneth. "Top 10 China Dependent Countries." *Forbes*. Forbes Inc. Nov 26 2015. Web. 26 Apr 2016.

Velez-Hagan, Justin. *The Common Sense Behind Basic Economics: A Guide for Budding Economists*. New York: Lexington Books, 2015. Pg 111.

Wong, Edward. "U.S. Case Offers Glimpse Into China's Hacker Army." *New York Times*. New York Times Company. May 22 2014. Web. 20 Apr 2016.

"World Economic Outlook (WEO) Update." *IMF*. International Monetary Fund. Jan 2016. Pdf. 20 Apr 2016.

Zimmerman, James. "Stalled Chinese Reforms, Stalled Chinese Economy." *Wall Street Journal*. Dow Jones & Company. Apr 13 2016. Web. 20 Apr 2016.

Notes

1. Callen, "Gross Domestic Product: An Economy's All."
2. "World Economic Outlook Update," *IMF*.
3. Monaghan, "China Surpasses US as World's Largest Trading Nation."

4. Esposito and Tse, "China Is Expanding Its Economic Influence in Africa. What Is Africa Getting Out of It?"

5. Rapoza, "Top 10 China Dependent Countries."

6. Gillespie, "China Contagion: How it Ripples Across the World."

7. Velez-Hagan, "The Common Sense Behind Basic Economics," Pg 111.

8. "FACT SHEET: U.S.-China Economic Relations," *White House*.

9. "China's 8-7 National Poverty Reduction Program," *World Bank*.

10. "China 2030: Building a Modern, Harmonious, and Creative Society," *The World Bank*.

11. Zimmerman, "Stalled Chinese Reforms, Stalled Chinese Economy."

China's Two Big Economic Challenges

By John Cassidy
The New Yorker, January 12, 2016

The renewed turbulence in China's stock markets—on Monday, the Shanghai exchange closed down more than five per cent—highlights the dual challenges facing the government in Beijing. The first task is restoring some stability to the country's notoriously volatile markets. The second challenge, which is of much greater importance, is fixing the Chinese economy, which, for a couple of years now, has been looking a bit like Wile E. Coyote—stepping off a cliff and hovering in the air for a while, legs pumping furiously to defy gravity.

From the rest of the world's perspective, this is the key issue. China's stock market is still relatively small, and even if it were to crash again, the spillovers wouldn't be very great. But the Chinese economy is now the world's second largest, and its recent troubles have already caused a lot of turbulence, especially in the commodity markets. A full-on slump in China would have huge global ramifications.

To some extent, the gyrations in the markets reflect policy errors that can be rectified. When it decided to divide responsibility for overseeing the stock market and the currency markets between two different institutions, the China Securities Regulatory Commission and the People's Bank of China, the government in Beijing was following Western best practices. Over the past week, however, the two overseers have sent conflicting signals to investors, undermining confidence, and, possibly, creating a negative feedback loop between the two markets.

As with many big market movements, it is difficult to identify one particular trigger. Stocks started falling right after New Year's, when some fresh data confirmed that China's vast manufacturing sector is shrinking. Fears that the regulatory commission was about to end a ban on selling by major shareholders, which was introduced during last summer's market swoon, may also have played a role. So, perhaps, did perceptions that the Chinese central bank was trying to engineer a devaluation in the currency, the renminbi, against the U.S. dollar, which could help out the country's exporters. And finally, the presence of "circuit breakers"—halts in trading when the market falls by a certain amount—may have added to the selloff rather than diminishing it.

At this stage, it would help to have a message from somebody with real authority that the Chinese government understands the need for coördination and is taking steps to bring it about. Various state agencies appear to be operating at cross purposes, and the country's leadership seems stuck between a desire to allow market forces to exert themselves and a nagging fear of what those forces might produce—in this case, violent swings in stock prices.

In the United States, as we saw in 2008, the job of reassuring the markets would rest with the Treasury Secretary and the head of the Federal Reserve. In China, where the policymaking apparatus is more opaque, the onus may fall on Premier Li Keqiang, who oversees economic policy and economic reforms; Zhou Xiaochuan, the longtime head of the central bank; or a lesser official. As is now glaringly obvious, the situation presents challenges to a Communist government that is used to pulling levers behind the scenes. Markets need clear guidance—even if the guidance is that the state is adopting a laissez-faire approach.

Since the Chinese government includes some very smart people, it shouldn't be beyond it to fashion a common front, which could include a commitment to further institutional reforms. Even before this week, there was talk in Beijing of creating a super-regulator to improve coördination, or aping what Britain did after 2008 and handing more power to the central bank. But lining up the regulatory apparatus is the easy bit.

As I said up top, the real challenge is dealing with the rest of the economy. After more than two decades of tremendous growth, practically everybody acknowledges that China faces some serious problems: chronic overcapacity in many manufacturing industries; very high levels of debt, particularly in the corporate sector; the aftermath of a real-estate bubble in some parts of the country; and a rapid demographic transition that means the working-age population is now declining. Based on the history of other rapidly growing developing countries, a full-on bust would appear to be a real threat.

China optimists—the sensible ones, anyway—don't diminish the scale of the task. Rather, they note that the Chinese government has been well aware of the problems for years and has been making some progress. Employment in the services sector is growing. Some of the shadow banks, which were lending money pell-mell, have been reined in. Officials are talking of allowing large state-owned companies to go bankrupt. Over the past year, to cushion the effects of the downturn in manufacturing, they have cut interest rates and accelerated infrastructure projects.

According to official figures, these policy moves have kept the Chinese economy growing; indeed, the growth rate of G.D.P. hasn't fallen much below the official target of seven per cent. Household spending has held up surprisingly well. House prices are rebounding in some cities. In a forecast for the *Economist*, Simon Rabinovitch, the magazine's Asian economics editor (who is always worth reading), wrote that 2016 would be the year when the skeptics conceded that "although China's turbo-charged days are over, its growth is not about to evaporate."

That prediction might turn out to be accurate. However, this week's turbulence is a timely reminder that the skeptics also have some powerful arguments. The renewed dive in the stock market, although it was accentuated by policy errors, may reflect a more fundamental factor: a lack of confidence in the Chinese economy. Despite the fact that some of the largest Chinese companies are now trading at relatively modest multiples of their earnings, local investors evidently believe that they are still overvalued.

Manufacturing, the primary motor of the Chinese miracle, continues to sputter, as does construction, another key driver of the boom. At least some of the recent growth in service-sector employment was in financial services, and was probably linked to the stock-market bubble, which has now burst for a second time. Looking at the economy as a whole, the rate of inflation has fallen from more than five per cent five years ago to 1.5 per cent in December. It is pretty obvious that there is a serious shortage of aggregate demand, which is depressing prices and generating a threat of deflation.

For those of us who place a lot of stock in debt cycles, it is also worrying that the overall debt-to-G.D.P. ratio continues to climb—some estimates put it at two hundred and forty per cent—and that a large-scale restructuring of bad debts, which will surely be necessary at some point, continues to be postponed. ("Balance sheets and credit quality have deteriorated in sectors with excess capacity," a new analysis by the World Bank notes.) One lesson of past crises is that it is almost always better, and less costly, to deal with debt problems early.

Finally, the reputation for competence of the Chinese authorities, which was hard-earned, has again been called into question. I don't agree with those observers, such as CNBC's Jim Cramer, who claim that the Chinese don't know what they are doing. I do doubt that the country will succeed without resorting to more radical policy measures, such as bigger doses of fiscal stimulus, further interest-rate cuts, corporate-debt restructurings, and a significant devaluation of the currency. Each of these options, in turn, could generate further financial instability. In any case, we will be reading a lot more about what happens in China this year.

Beijing Inc?: The Chinese Aren't Coming—They're Here

By Roland Flamini

World Affairs, November/December 2014

This past Labor Day, a great many of the sausages consumed at cookouts across the country came from Smithfield Foods Inc., formerly the US food giant, but for the past year a wholly owned subsidiary of China's Shuanghui International Holdings. Shuanghui paid $4.7 billion for Smithfield, whose operation spans hog farms and pork processing facilities in more than a dozen states, including Virginia, Maryland, North Carolina, and Wisconsin. The deal was China's largest single investment in the United States to date, and helped boost Chinese mergers, acquisitions, and "greenfield projects" (companies setting up their own factories) to a record $14 billion by the end of 2013. Despite bilateral tensions over cyber espionage, Chinese territorial disputes with America's allies in the South China Sea, and the slow progress of China's massive economic reforms—and despite increasing calls for more scrutiny from Congress—China Inc closed a total of eight hundred and seventy-nine major deals last year across the American map, from New Jersey to California.

The US Chamber of Commerce approved. "The evolution from a one-way to a two-way investment relationship is good news for the US and can help stabilize and deepen US-China relations," it declared in a 2014 study on the continued flow of Chinese capital into the United States. The Obama administration clearly agrees that China's direct investments can have a positive influence on the Sino-American bilateral strategic and economic dialogue, and has gone out of its way to attract it.

But the optimism is far from universal. The sharp expansion of Chinese investments has stirred considerable unease among US lawmakers on both sides of the aisle. There is concern about the possible damage to US security and economic interests and skepticism about China's long-term intentions. Is this stepped-up financial activity an elaborate scheme to take proprietary technology out of the US, by moving R&D to China, with a resulting loss of American jobs? That these aggressive Chinese investing firms operate under an authoritarian political regime adds another layer of worry to what some see as a slow-motion financial invasion.

Earlier this year, the US-China Economic and Security Review Commission, established by Congress in 2000 to monitor the bilateral relationship, warned in a report that the huge, rich, and powerful Chinese state-owned enterprises "are not pure market actors and may be driven by state goals, not market forces." It goes on to say "these entities are potentially disruptive because they frequently respond to policies of the Chinese government," and thus Chinese investments can function as "a potential Trojan horse."

Chinese investment is one issue that can unite an otherwise deeply divided Congress. In an early skirmish in 2005, Congress closed ranks to prevent the China National Offshore Oil Corporation from acquiring Unocal Corporation of California for $18.5 billion because of "security considerations." The Chinese energy giant—the subsidiary of a state-owned Chinese petroleum enterprise—withdrew its offer, citing "unprecedented political oppression."

Since then, the congressional focus has been on possible Chinese attacks on US technology. Recently, the chairman and the ranking member of the House Permanent Select Committee on Intelligence, Representatives Mike Rogers of Michigan and C. A. Dutch Ruppersberger of Maryland, took aim at Huawei Technologies Co., the Chinese version of Twitter, with more than one hundred and forty million users, and ZTE Corp., one of the world's biggest smartphone vendors. The two congressmen reached across the aisle to recommend that "acquisitions, takeovers, and mergers involving Huawei and ZTE" be blocked, "given the threat to national security interests." The lawmakers said they had "serious concerns about Huawei and ZTE, and their connection to the communist government of China . . . a major perpetrator of cyber espionage."

In July 2010, fifty members of the Congressional Steel Caucus signed a letter to the administration calling for a thorough investigation of the Chinese state-owned Anshan Iron and Steel Group Corporation's plans to invest in steel plants owned by the Steel Development Company of Mississippi, which, the letter said, could give the Chinese "access to new steel production techniques and information regarding American national security infrastructure projects." And when three state-owned Chinese banks planned to open branches in the United States, Pennsylvania Democratic Senator Bob Casey wrote to then Federal Reserve Chairman Ben Bernanke expressing his concern that the banks "will use their state support as a way to underprice US banks that abide by US law."

According to research prepared earlier this year for Congress by the Congressional Research Service, when the US subsidiary of China's Wanxiang Group acquired A123 Systems Inc., whose products include special battery packs for US soldiers, "several members of Congress expressed concerns over the national security implications . . . as well as concerns that US government grants that had been given to A123 Systems in the past might end up benefitting a Chinese company."

Such opposition has not stopped the trend that has continued this year, with real estate, high-tech, manufacturing, and unconventional energy sectors the big draws. In New York, real estate developer Zhang Xin's Soho China Ltd. shared, with a Middle Eastern developer, the purchase of a forty-percent stake in the General Motors Building, a Manhattan landmark, each paying $1.4 billion. In the high-tech sector, IBM's sale of its low-end server business, x86, to the Chinese PC maker Lenovo Group Ltd. for $2.3 billion has grabbed headlines. Yuhuang Chemical Inc. is set to begin construction of a methanol manufacturing complex in St. James Parish, on the Mississippi River in Louisiana, and, in the biggest greenfield project by a Chinese company in the United States to date, the Shandong Tranlin Paper Co. is investing $2 billion in setting up a manufacturing operation in a suburb of Richmond, Virginia. According to market analysts at the Rhodium Group, which tracks Chinese investment in the US, there are more than $10 billion worth of deals currently pending.

With its huge pile of foreign currency reserves and need for resources, an increase in overseas investments was a natural next step in China's economic development. The push was both government-mandated and driven by changing commercial realities at home that forced Chinese companies to function in an increasingly high-priced and regulated domestic environment. Beijing created sovereign wealth funds, and in 1996 introduced what it called a "going out" strategy, urging firms to go after overseas investments. Chinese firms responded like racehorses out of a starting gate, with the United States as the number one finishing post.

Originally, "going out" was all about securing natural resources to continue China's growth. But the acquisition of Smithfield reflects how Chinese investor interest has broadened in the past five years, looking beyond fossil fuels or metal ores. Wan Long, Shuanghui's combative chairman, said his motives for acquiring Smithfield were "to assemble the most advanced technology, unmatched resources, and outstanding talents in the pork industry." It is no mystery what Shuanghui expects out of the deal: Western expertise to give them a competitive edge, both at home and internationally, a springboard to foreign markets, including the US market, and strong brand identity.

In comparative terms, Chinese investment in the US to date is still small. China doesn't even make the top fifteen countries on the US Department of Commerce list of foreign direct investors for 2012 (the most recent figures available). The Chinese investment total for that year was $10.45 billion, well below the United Kingdom, with $564.7 billion, and Japan, a distant second, with $309.3 billion.

Inevitably, opposition to China's plunge into the US has revived memories of Japan's investment frenzy in the United States in the late 1980s, when Japanese conglomerates, using their excess export dollars, snapped up American companies, property, and movie studios—causing a fearful and openly xenophobic opposition. There was also the fact that the Japanese kept their own market closed to US investments and limited American exports in key industrial sectors. By 1989, Japanese corporate mergers and acquisitions reached $20 billion. At the time, Mitsubishi's acquisition of Rockefeller Center, Sony's takeover of Columbia Pictures, and Matsushita's purchase of MCI Universal Studios were highlights of Japan's investment offensive. Amid an orgy of "Japanese bashing" in the media, White House economic adviser Lawrence Summers warned that Japan was "a greater threat to the US than the Soviet Union."

But the massive Japanese spending spree was based on unrealistic projections of growth and returns, and even as US opposition calmed and many of Japan's transplanted manufacturers gained a measure of acceptance, with Japanese employment of Americans growing to six hundred thousand, the Japanese stock market crashed in 1987 and the financial bubble burst at home, causing nearly two decades of economic stagnation and a turnabout in America. The bankruptcy of Rockefeller Center, whose purchase by Japan was once seen as a symbol of financial conquest, became in turn a symbol of financial defeat.

Japan Inc's adventure in America is a cautionary tale for the Chinese. But it is unlikely that this piece of economic history will be repeated.

Beijing does place limits on foreign investment, but trade with China is very much a two-way street, with a lot at stake for both countries. China is America's third-largest export market, and US investments in China are worth $51.4 billion. From 2010 to 2013, General Motors sold more vehicles in China than it did in the home market. China's cumulative investment in the US is $36.5 billion and growing, and the Obama administration is happy "to welcome, encourage, and see nothing but positive benefit from direct investment in the United States from Chinese businesses and Chinese entities," as Vice President Joe Biden said recently. And while Chinese intentions continue to be questioned by policymakers and politicians, Chinese investment is seen as a godsend by states and cities with high unemployment and strained budgets.

Congressional concern has focused on the Committee on Foreign Investment in the United States (CFIUS), the shadowy interagency body set up in 1975 that acts as gatekeeper for incoming foreign investment. Since it was established by President Gerald Ford, CFIUS has been re-shaped a number of times, but its essential role of screening potential foreign investment inflows for any significant danger to US interests and national security remains the same.

In its present form, the committee is chaired by the secretary of the Treasury and includes as members the secretaries of State, Homeland Security, Defense, Commerce, and Energy, the attorney general, the US trade representative, the director of the Office of Science and Technology Policy, the director of National Intelligence, and the director of the National Security Council. The Foreign Investment and National Security Act (FINSA) of 2007 brought CFIUS under closer congressional control. The bipartisan legislation made it mandatory for the agency to conduct an investigation of all proposed investments involving firms owned by a foreign government. CFIUS must also report to the Senate Banking Committee and the House Financial Services Committee on the result of all its investigations, file an annual report, and advise senators and representatives of foreign investment in businesses in their respective districts.

> **The sharp expansion of Chinese investments has stirred considerable unease among US lawmakers on both sides of the aisle. There is concern about the possible damage to US security and economic interests and skepticism about China's long-term intentions.**

Subsequent proposals from lawmakers at a 2014 hearing of the US-China Economic and Security Review Commission included a new "net economic benefit test" to determine what's in a given deal for the United States, and including scrutiny where appropriate of greenfield investments, which so far are exempt from the CFIUS. (Neither proposal has as yet been incorporated into the CFIUS screening process.)

"The CFIUS process is entirely confidential before, during, and after," says attorney John Bellinger III of the Washington law firm of Arnold & Porter, who has been dealing with the committee both inside and outside the government for almost twenty years. Still, more and more Chinese businesses are seeking Congress's reaction before the CFIUS process. "It's a delicate balance because on the one hand you don't want to raise the level of [congressional] awareness, on the other hand you don't want members of Congress to read about a transaction in the papers and immediately have a negative reaction. You have to ask, how much defensive briefing should I do with Congress?"

For example, in August, when Huawei's bid to buy 3Leaf Systems (an insolvent technology firm) drew protests from the Hill before the CFIUS screening process, on the grounds that the deal would put advanced American computer technology in Chinese hands, the company withdrew its application.

But what is "sensitive" in potential Chinese purchases of American enterprises? The FINSA legislation redefined "national security" to include infrastructure, and after further additions post-9/11, seventeen sectors of the economy now fall within the definition of critical infrastructure/key resources. But the net can be cast even wider. In September 2012, when President Obama cited national security interests in ordering the Chinese-owned Ralls Corporation to divest its interest in Oregon wind farms (one of the company sites was too close to a US Navy air base where drones were tested), it was the first time in more than two decades that a US president had exercised the authority given him in the screening process to block a deal acting on the recommendation of the interagency committee. In the same vein, CFIUS has rejected three successive bids by different Chinese mining companies to invest in mining operations in Nevada because in every instance the mine was judged to be too close to Fallon Naval Air Station in Nevada's Lahontan Valley.

As the scope of Chinese investments becomes broader, new questions arise. The Smithfield Foods acquisition brought a torrent of protest from the Hill. During the CFIUS review process, fifteen members of the Senate Committee on Agriculture, Nutrition, and Forestry protested that the US food supply was "critical infrastructure" with national security implications, and should not be sold to a foreign power. Then, at the committee hearing when the sale went through, the chair, Michigan Democrat Debbie Stabenow, summed up the prevailing sentiment: "We need to evaluate how foreign purchases of our food supply will affect our economy broadly, and frankly, whether there is a level playing field when it comes to these kinds of business purchases. Could this sale happen if it were the other way around? Could Smithfield purchase Shuanghui? Based on what we've heard from many experts already, it sounds like the answer is no."

In fact, there has been little reciprocity in the way China treats American business organizations. Despite making enormous progress in the past decade, says Shaun Donnelly, vice president for investment at the US Council for International Business, an influential business advocacy group, "China has not yet established an open, market-based investment regime. Far from it: screenings, controls, restrictions, informal pressures, and political interventions remain central to the Chinese investment system." Major areas of concern expressed by US policymakers and businessmen include China's extensive use of financial subsidies for state-owned enterprises; trade and investment barriers, including business sectors closed to foreign investors; pressure on foreign firms in China to transfer technology as the price for market access, in order to give Chinese firms a competitive edge; a relatively poor record of respecting intellectual property rights and keeping its currency undervalued; poor marks in respecting and implementing World Trade Organization obligations; and, of course, a record of hacking US government offices and businesses.

What both Washington and Beijing say they want is a bilateral investment treaty, which Obama and Chinese President Xi Jinping put on the fast track at their California summit in 2013. In July, the two sides committed to reach agreement on the core text by the end of 2014. The American side wants to see China open off-limits sectors in the Chinese economy to foreign investors through a significant reduction of the so-called "negative list," which currently covers one hundred and thirty-nine separate areas, including finance and real estate. The Chinese complain that, while America claims to be open to outside investment, its own negative list has been growing.

In reality, the US position is deeply ambivalent. While federal officials worry about the impact of Chinese investments, state and local officials work hard to attract China's business organizations. So the contest for China's investment dollars is fought at state and city levels where what makes the difference are local infrastructure, industry clusters, state and local tax holidays, access to thriving markets, proximity to universities and research laboratories, human resource pools, local union attitudes, and labor laws.

At least thirty US states have established offices in the People's Republic of China to promote trade and investment. The governors of California, Virginia, and Illinois among others have journeyed to China at the head of trade delegations to sell their respective states, and Chinese businessmen often receive VIP treatment when they visit America. California's capital, Sacramento, where the highest number by far of Chinese firms is concentrated (two hundred and thirty-six at the most recent count), has established its own presence to drum up investments and increase trade generally in both Shanghai and China's most populous city, Chongqing, which, says Antonio Yung, who runs this office for Sacramento, "is an up and coming area where we can operate with less competition [than they would face in Shanghai]." One challenge these trade offices face is to dispel what Bellinger calls "skittishness" among Chinese businessmen about investment in the US "because of their awareness of high profile rejections. Certain areas—cyber areas, technological areas, areas where they are in physical proximity to US defense locations—are going to get a lot of scrutiny and get turn downs, but ninety percent of acquisitions are going to go through." Unlike the inflamed situation that accompanied the Japanese "invasion" of three decades ago, there are no reports of tensions in China's workplaces in America or prolonged labor disputes. Although the workforce in Chinese-owned establishments is around seventy thousand, Beijing's capital inflow may have saved jobs, since some of the acquisitions involved companies with poor financial balance sheets. A123 Systems was bankrupt. In 2010, Pacific Century Motors of China bought Nexteer, a Michigan auto parts maker, saving thousands of jobs in Saginaw, Michigan. "This city went from being an exhibit of America's industrial decline to a case study of the impact of Chinese investment money on a US community," the *Wall Street Journal* wrote.

Some economists claim that in return for creating jobs in the US, the Chinese will learn the benefits of working in an environment of rules and justice. In August, Chinese investing companies in America had a demonstration of how businesses are protected under the rule of law when the Court of Appeals in Washington halted a presidential order to the Ralls Corporation to divest itself of its Oregon wind farms on the grounds that the Chinese company's constitutional rights had not been respected. The court ruled that Ralls had a right to due process, which in this instance meant access to unclassified information that had led to the agency's decision, plus the right to rebut the evidence. The court had also left open the question whether CFIUS had exceeded its authority. Ironically, none of the Chinese media that hailed the court decision considered whether such a decision would be possible in their own country.

Can China's Companies Conquer the World?: The Overlooked Importance of Corporate Power

By Pankaj Ghemawat and Thomas Hout
Foreign Affairs, March/April 2016

Despite China's recent economic struggles, many economists and analysts argue that the country remains on course to overtake the United States and become the world's leading economic power someday soon. Indeed, this has become a mainstream view—if not quite a consensus belief—on both sides of the Pacific. But proponents of this position often neglect to take into account an important truth: economic power is closely related to business power, an area in which China still lags far behind the United States.

To understand how that might affect China's future prospects, it's important to first grasp the reasons why many remain bullish on China—to review the evidence that supports the case for future Chinese dominance. At first glance, the numbers are impressive. China's GDP is likely to surpass that of the United States—although probably not until at least 2028, which is five to ten years later than most analysts were predicting before China's current slowdown began in 2014. After all, China is already the world's largest market for hundreds of products, from cars to power stations to diapers. The Chinese government has over $3 trillion in foreign exchange reserves, which is easily the world's largest such holding. And China overshadows the United States in trade volume: of the 180 nations with which the two countries both trade, China is the larger trading partner with 124, including some important U.S. political and military allies. Finally, China has made steady progress toward its goal of becoming the investor, infrastructure builder, equipment supplier, and banker of choice in the developing world. Much of Asia, Africa, and Latin America now depends on China economically and politically.

Since Chinese share prices tumbled last summer and then again earlier this year, investors have grown wary of the country's stock market. But that market has been largely irrelevant to China's economic growth: from 1990 to 2013, as Chinese GDP grew at roughly ten percent annually, the stock market barely moved. Its recent gyrations are no more indicative of China's overall economic well-being than was its long stagnation. China will likely recover from its current economic setbacks just as the United States recuperated after wild stock market swings and a major depression in the first half of the twentieth century.

But strong macroeconomic data don't tell the whole story, and China's likely short-term recovery will mean little in the longer run. The fact is that China's success to date doesn't necessarily mean that it will surpass the United States as the world's leading economic power. Metrics such as GDP, trade volume, and financial reserves all reflect economic power. But they don't entirely encompass it, for underneath those numbers lies the real world of corporations and industries that actually create growth and wealth. And a close look at the performance and prospects of Chinese firms reveals the obstacles the country still faces.

In both China and the United States, corporations account for roughly three-quarters of GDP. More generally, multinational corporations and their supply chains control 80 percent of global exports and foreign direct investment. In other words, economic power rests heavily on business power.

China's economy exploded during the last three decades thanks to the extraordinary performance of its low-cost manufacturers—reliable, responsive companies that make the apparel and household items that fill Walmart's shelves. The Chinese state created the conditions for such firms to thrive by upgrading China's infrastructure, attracting foreign investment, and keeping the value of China's currency relatively low. But to succeed, Chinese manufacturers still had to outperform competitors elsewhere—which they did, turning China into a crucial player on the global economic stage.

If China is ever going to become the world's most powerful economy, however, its businesses will have to learn to excel in the much more competitive capital-goods and high-tech sectors, creating and marketing sophisticated products such as semiconductors, medical imaging equipment, and jet aircraft. Those who believe that China will become dominant often assume that Chinese firms will perform as well in those second-generation sectors as they have in far less complex first-generation ones, such as textiles and consumer electronics. But there are many reasons to question that assumption.

China's initial economic boom relied on labor outsourcing by U.S. and European firms and revolved around hundreds of similar companies, many of them foreign-owned, that exported low-tech products. In contrast, to succeed in capital goods (goods that are used to produce other goods) and high technology, companies must develop unique capabilities suited to a small number of clients, master a broad range of technologies, acquire deep customer knowledge, and manage a global supply chain. And unlike in the low-cost manufacturing sector, where Chinese firms have competed primarily with companies in developing countries, the capital-goods and high-tech industries are dominated by large, deep-pocketed multinational corporations based in Japan, South Korea, the United States, and Europe.

Moreover, some of the advantages that China enjoyed during the past three decades, such as a large labor force, matter less in determining whether a country succeeds in capital goods and high technology. For example, jet aircraft production and Internet [searches] are led by two companies—Boeing and Google, respectively—that are based in a large country, the United States. But the leading companies in high-precision bearings (SKF) and semiconductor memory chips (Samsung) are based in much smaller countries: Sweden and South Korea, respectively. The roots of those companies' success lie mostly inside the firms themselves rather than in advantages conferred by their host countries.

The future of China's economic power will depend less on when the country's GDP passes that of the United States and more on the progress that Chinese corporations make in manufacturing and selling capital goods and high technology. Foreign multinationals still dominate China's home market in advanced capital goods, and China remains broadly dependent on Western technology. In the areas that will matter most in the twenty-first century, Chinese companies have a long way to go, which should give pause to anyone confidently predicting a not-too-distant era of Chinese economic dominance.

Downstream vs. Upstream

Although it is still playing catch-up, China has made some significant progress in its quest to move into capital goods and high-tech products, which now account for 25 percent of its exports. Chinese producers currently control between 50 and 75 percent of the global markets (including China) for shipping containers, port cranes, and coal power generation equipment and between 15 and 30 percent of the global markets for telecommunications equipment, onshore wind turbines, and high-speed rail systems. Despite rising wages and energy costs, Chinese firms have used their ability to simplify manufacturing processes to maintain a ten to 30 percent cost advantage over Western competitors in capital goods—even before the recent devaluation of the yuan.

The Chinese government's trillion-dollar "One Belt, One Road" strategy, which aims to cover the Eurasia with Chinese-built roads, rail, and port facilities, gives Chinese producers additional advantages far from home. The government has also aided local firms by limiting the amounts of capital goods and services that major Western companies can sell in China and by requiring them to transfer technologies to Chinese companies. Still, China has yet to become a real player in the markets for more expensive and complex products, such as offshore wind turbines, nuclear reactor cores, and large jet aircraft. As the head of a large Western aviation manufacturer remarked to us recently, it is one thing to reverse engineer the components of a jet engine and figure out how to make and sell them, but quite another to develop the knowledge and skills to make sure those components actually work together.

Chinese capabilities tend to be oriented "downstream": absorbing imported technologies, simplifying manufacturing, and adapting advanced designs to more basic products at a lower cost. Such tinkering and innovation at the margins has proved hugely beneficial for businesses that rely on mature technologies, such as shipping containers and port equipment. But Western multinationals tend to focus their energies "upstream": on developing deep knowledge of customers' technical needs, designing high-performing products that incorporate new technologies, and mastering software development and the efficient management of global supply chains. Those qualities have allowed Western companies to dominate the markets for nuclear power reactors, industrial automation systems, and jet aircraft. Chinese companies have been slow to develop upstream skills, which partly explains why their success in capital-goods and high-tech markets has been uneven and why it's unclear how soon they will be able to move from the lower end to the higher end of those sectors.

Competition from Western firms has slowed the growth in exports of Chinese-made telecommunications equipment from 25 percent in 2010 to ten percent in 2014. Meanwhile, China accounts for only around 15 percent of global exports in infrastructure contractor services—a number that hasn't grown in five years. Its overall export growth slowed from an average annual increase of 17 percent between 2004 and 2011 to an average annual increase of five percent between 2011 and 2015, and the share of exports accounted for by capital goods has leveled off at 25 percent. China is not transitioning from low-end, first-generation exports to high-end, second-generation exports as quickly as Japan or South Korea did. When those countries' GDPs per capita were at China's current level, capital goods made up more than 25 percent of their exports, and their performance on capital-goods exports continued to improve, rather than leveling off as China's has.

In addition to their relative lack of upstream skills, Chinese firms also face challenges when it comes to managing global supply chains. Chinese companies have typically tried to reduce costs by learning to manufacture critical components, such as hydraulics for construction equipment or avionics for jet aircraft, so that they can avoid importing them. Most Western companies take a different approach, turning to multiple sources for such parts: suppliers from all over Asia and Europe provide components for Apple iPhones and Boeing 787s, for example. These contrasting sourcing patterns reflect different views of how to create business power and also demonstrate China's historical preoccupation with self-sufficiency. Chinese authorities invite more advanced foreign companies into China, learn from them, and try to replace them, whereas Western multinationals prefer to find the best available components no matter where they originate. The difference will allow China to develop a larger production scale, but its foreign competitors will be able to draw from a bigger, more competitive pool of partners.

Inspect Their Gadgets

China is a particularly interesting place to look at the head-to-head competition between Chinese companies and foreign multinationals, both because it's the world's largest market for most products and because nearly every major company in the world operates there. Unsurprisingly, out of a representative sample of 44 industries among those that are open to foreign corporations in China, Chinese companies dominate 25, including solar panels, construction equipment, and mobile port cranes. But in all of the 19 sectors led by foreign multinationals, technology or marketing is disproportionately critical to success. Foreign multinationals operating in China lead in ten of the 13 industries in which R & D costs are greater than six percent of revenue, including jet aircraft, packaged software, and semiconductors.

And foreign firms lead in four of the six industries in which advertising costs exceed six percent of revenue, including carbonated beverages, patented pharmaceuticals, and personal-care and beauty products.

Another striking thing about the Chinese market is how little the industry leaders have changed over the last decade. During this period, Chinese companies displaced foreign firms as leaders in only two of the 44 industries in question: Internet hardware (including a portion of the wireless telecommunications sector) and wind turbines. And in the latter case, China's industrial policy tilted the playing field by limiting foreign producers' access to the market and by requiring them to use many Chinese-manufactured parts.

Meanwhile, little evidence supports the widespread notion that China is the world's leading exporter of high-tech gadgets. Although China does lead the world in the export of smartphones and personal computers, it accounts for only 15 percent of those products' value at most. That's because Chinese companies typically just assemble and package semiconductors, software, cameras, and other advanced high-tech components fabricated abroad. Consider the Tianhe-2, for example. This supercomputer, built by the Chinese firm Inspur in collaboration with the National University of Defense Technology, is the fastest in the world. But it is only Chinese in a very limited sense, since it is actually composed of thousands of U.S.-made microprocessors.

Playing Catch-Up

The dominance of Western multinationals in capital goods and high technology rests on two pillars: open systems of innovation that result in superior high-performance products and direct foreign investment in operations that are global in scale but responsive to local conditions and needs. If they ever hope to challenge the industry leaders, Chinese firms will have to develop their own versions of those qualities. Some have taken steps in that direction, but their lack of experience in designing advanced systems and managing international supply chains will likely limit what they can do for many years.

The superior commercial technology currently enjoyed by foreign incumbents will be one of the major obstacles China faces. In 2014, China spent $218 billion to import semiconductors, far more than it spent on crude oil. It also paid $21 billion in royalties for the use of foreign-owned technologies, a number that has doubled since 2008 and that rankles Beijing. (It hardly helps that the government's own information systems are dependent on technology made by IBM, Oracle, EMC, Qualcomm, and other non-Chinese firms, which many Chinese officials see as a security problem.)

Last year, Beijing launched a serious drive, called "Made in China 2025," to transform the country into an innovative and environmentally responsible "world manufacturing power" within ten years. The program aims to create 40 innovation centers in ten sectors, including smart transportation, information technology, and aerospace. If the government follows through, China's total public and private spending on R & D may well surpass that of the United States sometime in the next ten years—a significant milestone even if one takes into account the high levels of fraud in Chinese research and the fact that Chinese government research funds are frequently misallocated to serve political agendas. The increase in funding has already had one easily observable effect: papers published by Chinese researchers are gaining more international respect. China's share of the papers recognized in Thomson Reuters' authoritative Science Citation Index rose from near zero in 2001 to 9.5 percent in 2011, putting the country second only to the United States.

But R & D spending is far from the only factor that matters. Succeeding in capital goods and high-tech equipment results from a long chain of institutional, social, and legal supports. At the front end of the chain lie high-quality graduate-degree programs, an open flow of information through peer-reviewed journals, and reliable protections for intellectual property; at the back end are advanced product design, innovative engineering, and frequent collaboration with important customers. The United States excels at each part of that chain. It boasts superior graduate programs in stem subjects (science, technology, engineering, and math) that attract the best students from all over the world, with China and India by far the largest sources. (Despite all the attention paid to the fact that many Chinese students return home after getting their U.S. degrees, stem students from China are actually more likely to stay in the United States than stem grads from anywhere else.) U.S. federal nondefense spending on research has been flat for the last ten years, but American corporations—which fund nearly three-quarters of total U.S. R & D—increased their research spending by an average of 3.5 percent annually during the same period. U.S. science journals produce a steady flow of peer-reviewed findings, and American scientists—unlike their Chinese counterparts—can profit from the intellectual property they produce during state-funded research. Many European and Japanese multinationals invest in research facilities in China, but the high degree of intellectual property protections in the United States lead them to base their most promising projects there.

To catch up, China is developing innovation and entrepreneurial hubs in Shenzhen and in Beijing's Zhongguancun Science Park. Shenzhen is home to a number of inventive companies, such as Huawei, Xiaomi, and DJI (China's leading drone manufacturer). But most of the firms clustered there focus on fast-turnaround, incremental innovations, not on big-ticket capital goods or high-tech products.

Barring major errors by Washington—for example, a failure to increase U.S. federal research funding—there is no reason to think the United States will lose its edge in technology. But if U.S. technology does stop advancing and Chinese competitors catch up, China's lower costs could allow it to gain market share. That's what happened in the case of equipment used in coal power generation: Chinese firms began to match their Western competitors in terms of quality and exploited their lower costs to become leaders in the global market. And even if Chinese wages continue to rise and the yuan begins to appreciate at some point, it's not likely that China will lose its cost advantage anytime soon. So if the United States wants to stay ahead, it has to keep winning in technology.

A Lonely Power

One of the keys to the United States' economic dominance is its huge investment in foreign markets. American corporations put $337 billion into overseas markets in 2014, a full ten percent of what they committed at home. All told, U.S. firms have directly invested $6.3 trillion overseas, which helps explain why the companies listed on the S&P 500 earn roughly 40 percent of their profits outside the United States. Despite slow growth at home, companies based in the United States and the EU have increased their foreign direct investment at an average annual rate of seven percent over the last ten years, and Japanese firms have increased theirs at an even faster rate.

After a late start, Chinese multinationals are now following this model. By the end of 2014, they had cumulatively invested $730 billion, and that number is projected to nearly triple, to $2 trillion, in the next five years—an impressive gain, although a figure that would still equal less than one-third of current U.S. foreign direct investment. Nearly all of China's early overseas investments were in oil fields and mines, but recently, Chinese corporations have begun moving up the value ladder by acquiring established Western companies or by purchasing and turning around struggling factories, some of them in the U.S. rust belt. China has made 141 overseas deals worth over $1 billion and is now home to more multinational enterprises than any country other than the United States.

But as a late globalizer, China has pursued a riskier foreign investment strategy than Western countries. Although Australia and the United States are the top two recipients of Chinese investment, over half of all Chinese foreign direct investment goes to developing countries in Asia, Africa, Latin America, and the Middle East. The riskier the country, the more willing the Chinese seem to be to put their money there. China is easily the largest foreign investor in Afghanistan, Angola, and Ecuador, for example—all places where wars or debt defaults have scared off most Westerners. The political scientist David Shambaugh has dubbed China "a lonely power," without close allies, and these investments, along with aid-financed public works projects and the much-touted Asian Infrastructure Investment Bank, are part of Beijing's strategy for changing that picture.

This approach might work. But in the meantime, Western multinationals are the primary investors in stable developing economies with stronger credit ratings and more democratic regimes, and they are profiting as a consequence. In 2014, the eu and Japan both invested more than China in Southeast Asia, and U.S. corporations alone invested $114 billion just in Asia (excluding Japan) and Latin America. The result of this strategy is that although China's bold investments attract considerable attention, Western and Japanese capital-goods and high-tech multinationals continue, with less fanfare, to expand their larger and more powerful global positions. China is a classic "late follower," investing in riskier assets and buying up second-tier Western technology companies. That might be a good way to play catch-up, but it is not a path to dominance.

A China Model?

Those who predict that China will dominate the future often point to two economic concepts to bolster their case: the product life cycle, which posits that a product originates in advanced economies but ends up being made in lower-cost developing economies, and disruptive innovation, the process by which leading products lose their position to initially inferior, lower-priced products that get better over time. But emphasizing these two trends overlooks the fact that incumbent multinationals can prevent those outcomes in capital goods and high technology by developing a range of products and supply chains in different regions and then mixing and matching them to serve different sets of customers around the globe.

Take, for example, Cummins, an Indiana-based U.S. diesel engine manufacturer that develops and manufactures product families with varying prices and different features in China, India, Europe, and North America. Cummins shares the lead in China's high-performance diesel engine sector, but its globally distributed production and R & D networks allow it to ship more engines into China than it ships out. Such global operations require cross-border coordination, technical depth in many locations, and middle managers with international experience.

Few Chinese firms enjoy those advantages. Most Chinese companies prefer to keep their production at home, use simple lines of organization, and maintain autonomy for the heads of individual businesses. That more stripped-down multinational model worked extremely well during China's first-generation boom. But in more recent years, many Chinese firms have struggled to adapt to globalization. There are exceptions, however: Lenovo, for example, passed Hewlett-Packard and Dell to become the world's largest personal computer manufacturer in 2013 by relying on an unusual international distribution of responsibilities, which involves foregoing a traditional global headquarters while centralizing the company's marketing operations in Bangalore, India.

> **The future of China's economic power will depend less on when the country's GDP passes that of the United States and more on the progress that Chinese corporations make in manufacturing and selling capital goods and high technology.**

Corporate China's uneven efforts to adapt to the global market will probably continue into the foreseeable future. In time, China will produce its share of great companies, just as other major economies have, but a unique "China model" seems unlikely to emerge, and it does not appear that the country's success rate will improve dramatically anytime soon.

A Long Climb For China

Advocates of the view that China will inevitably dominate the global economy tend to see the United States as strong but slow moving, owing to its messy free markets and political gridlock, and tend to see China as a rising power on the march, thanks to its clear planning and clever strategy. But this simplistic view fails to account for how corporations and markets change in response to external factors. U.S. business power flows from the restless competitiveness of American culture, the political influence of U.S. corporations, the research productivity of U.S. universities and government laboratories, a U.S. financial system that directs investment to new technologies and ventures, immigration that brings in talent, laws and tax codes that reward entrepreneurial activity, the United States' status as the sole superpower, and the dollar's role as the world's reserve currency.

There are internal factors that can threaten U.S. business power, of course—for example, right-wing opposition to federal science spending and activist shareholders' focus on the short-term profits of blue-chip firms instead of long-term investment in innovation. But 30 years ago, when some observers believed that Japan was poised to overtake the United States in terms of economic power, few predicted the role that tech entrepreneurs and innovative state and municipal governments would play in creating an era of unrivaled American dominance.

Chinese business power has different but also strong foundations, such as far-sighted policies favoring investment over consumption, government encouragement of foreign investment to jump-start local industries, intrepid entrepreneurs who succeed despite a state-enterprise system designed to thwart them, a shift in the world's center of economic gravity toward Asia, and a massive domestic market. Many factors hold China back, too, including a low-performing state-owned sector that stifles market forces, mounting internal debt burdens, and a crackdown on the free flow of information.

It's difficult to predict how external factors might influence the growth of Chinese economic power. Not many inside or outside China foresaw the limitations of state-owned enterprises or the rise of impressive independent firms such as Huawei, Lenovo, and Alibaba. Looking ahead, it's hard to know what effect China's slowing growth will have on the global competitiveness of its companies: it could prove deeply damaging, but it could also precipitate bankruptcies and industry shakeouts that would concentrate power in the hands of fewer, more capable companies, which could make them a stronger force in world markets.

More broadly, it's difficult to know how the rest of the world will respond to China as it grows. When China became a huge buyer of natural resources, many analysts fearfully predicted permanent increases in commodity prices. What happened instead was that prospectors found new ways to increase supply and governments and companies found new ways to conserve and improve efficiency. The global system adapted, and commodity prices overall are lower today in real terms than they were 20 years ago. In a similar vein, as Chinese multinationals fight their way into global markets, Western incumbents will innovate, consolidate, and develop new sources of demand.

Moreover, the futures of the U.S. and Chinese political systems are not fixed. Both have experienced remarkable adaptability as well as self-inflicted wounds, and there is no reason to think that will change.

Confidence in the inevitability of Chinese economic dominance is unfounded. China is gaining strength but faces a long climb. The outcome of the U.S.-Chinese contest is far from clear and depends at least as much on how well Western multinationals and governments exploit their existing advantages as on China's ability to up its game when it comes to the kinds of products and services that will define the twenty-first-century economy.

The Challenge: The Domestic Determinants of International Rivalry Between the United States and China

By David A. Lake

International Studies Review, September 1, 2014

Economic and political power within the international system is becoming more diffuse. Nonetheless, China is today the principal challenger to the United States. The European Union (EU) remains an economic powerhouse, but is currently plagued by problems centering on the euro and the austerity Germany and the fixed exchange rate regime have imposed on the continent. Europe has also shown little interest in challenging the United States in past decades and, in fact, has been a stalwart supporter of American hegemony for nearly 70 years. Japan remains the world's third largest economy and fourth largest trader, and after decades of stagnation may finally be on the road to economic recovery. Yet, it too remains a supporter of continued American leadership. Brazil, Russia, and India have garnered much attention recently but still rank low on the scale of economic power, whether measured by GDP or trade. China is the world's second largest economy and largest trader. By any measure, it is the only country likely to overtake the United States in the near future, although its ability to do so is not a foregone conclusion. The distribution of international power may soon return to bipolarity.

The challenge posed by China to the United States, however, arises not just from its emergence as a twenty-first-century superpower. In the past, hegemons have managed transitions by challengers without significant conflict, as when Britain ceded leadership over first the Western hemisphere and then all of the world economy to the United States (Lake 1988). Rather, the challenge—if it occurs— will emerge from fundamental differences in the domestic political economies of the United States and China. The United States is a liberal market economy in which prices are the primary determinant of the allocation of resources. China is a state market economy, increasingly controlled by narrow party elites and their families, in which politics determine resource allocation. The United States has successfully generalized its liberal market system to the international economy through seven decades of hegemony. The question for the future is whether integration into the American-led international economy will transform China's domestic political economy from statism to liberalism. If integration strengthens market forces within

China, cooperation between the two superpowers will likely be expanded as common interests prevail. If political forces remain dominant in China, greater conflict may emerge.

The American System

The United States is a liberal state in which political authority is highly decentralized in both government and society. With a limited and tightly constrained state, it relies primarily on market-based mechanisms to guide its economy. Public policy matters, of course, for the allocation of resources, but principally through tax and fiscal incentives that, in turn, condition the structure of relative prices. With many competing centers of economic power, reinforced by rules limiting monopolistic and anti-competitive practices, society responds relatively efficiently to price signals.

This liberal domestic political economy is constantly changing as technology and comparative advantage evolve, but it has retained its basic structure over time. That institutions are "sticky" is a commonplace observation, but not one that actually explains why structure endures. In my view, domestic structures are stable because social forces that benefit from the policies they produce develop interests in preserving those institutions and their privileged position within them. In turn, it is the domestic social interests vested in particular institutions that set states along a particular developmental path (Hall and Soskice 2001; Gourevitch and Shinn 2005). Liberal market economies, like the United States, have large spheres of private authority, rely more on market-based allocation systems, and offer fewer social protections. In turn, both firms and workers develop flexible economic strategies that discourage investments in specific processes or skills, creating a large pool of "generic" capital and labor that flows (relatively) easily across sectors. Having invested in flexible production and skills, however, society has little motivation to press the government for policies that encourage long-term holding of assets, apprenticeship programs tailored to long-term employment contracts, and other features common in "organized market economies" found in continental European states. Adapted for flexibility, changing policies are of less import in liberal market economies and the political arena is characterized by institutions that if they do not amplify at least do not dampen political swings, such as single-member electoral districts and majority party rule. The economy and its political actors are, thus, vested in a particular, self-reinforcing mode of production. The bottom line is that liberal market economies beget more liberal markets not because they are "institutionalized" but because social actors become vested into particular domestic structures.

The great innovation of American hegemony has been to externalize the liberal domestic economy of the United States onto the international economy, which has in turn gradually reshaped the domestic political economies of smaller states (Ikenberry 2001). Although vested interests make domestic structures hard to change, as in the United States, they are not immune to disruption. The "liberal project" of the United States after 1945 was greatly facilitated by the destruction of World War II and, especially, its postwar occupation of West Germany and Japan, two of the largest economic powers of their age. As defeated countries, West Germany and Japan were highly plastic after 1945. The war itself destroyed enormous economic assets, "divesting" domestic interests of much of their prior wealth and political interests. The old regimes were also delegitimized. The United States, in turn, dangled significant rewards before them if they would join the American-led international economy. This favored the rise of politically moderate, capitalist, and Western-oriented elites surrounding Konrad Adenauer in Germany and Shigeru Yoshida in Japan. Spreading the rewards of the American system broadly across the populations of these countries also brought the masses onboard and facilitated the consolidation of liberalism and democracy. In the end, it was an American empire, but it was an "empire by invitation" (Lundestad 1990).

Over time, states and more important societies within what Peter Katzenstein (2005) has called the "American imperium" have become vested in that unique international system. Groups develop interests in sustaining the international order to which they have adapted and prospered. In this way, the international order becomes self-enforcing. Imagine the political outcry from industries around the world that have adapted their production and sales to a global market if the World Trade Organization (WTO) were, say, to come under threat from protectionist forces. Previous collapses notwithstanding, globalization appears to have created interests sufficiently vested in economic openness that it is now a one-way bet, an observation supported by the near absence of protectionism in the Great Recession that began in 2008 (Kahler 2013). Free trade does not require homogenization of economies and polities, but does reward winners and punish losers, tilting the political playing field increasingly in favor of the former and against the latter (Rogowski 1989). Export interests and others that benefit from an open world economy gain, prosper, and expand their political influence. Import-competing sectors and others that lose steadily shrink in size and influence. Exporters become ever more dependent on

> **Examining China's domestic structure can give us some broad hints about its likely policy preferences and, thus, the potential for conflict with the United States.**

world markets and the national economy becomes increasingly specialized. These "internationalist" interests, in turn, develop stronger interests in maintaining market openness, both at home and abroad. International liberalism becomes self-sustaining and perhaps even expands. Thus, the American imperium has—slowly but inexorably—reshaped the domestic political economies of its members, an effect that is deeper and more dramatic the higher the level of integration. This has created, over time, a highly robust and even "institutionalized" international system.

The Rise of China

As China becomes more powerful in the decades ahead, it is widely expected to challenge the United States because it can or because it favors a different package of policies and international economic rules, although the content of this package is typically left unspecified. That China will overtake the United States is often taken as given, with analysts only differing on the timing. But China's rise is by no means a certainty. One need only remember the fear of "Japan, Inc." in the 1980s—an overhyped trend that was followed by an American technological resurgence and two decades of stagnation in Japan—to know that long-term predictions of national growth can often be wrong. Much could change in China and elsewhere that would alter its current trajectory. Equally important, however, even pessimists do not have a good theory or empirical foundation for predicting what a stronger China will want in international politics. Examining China's domestic structure can give us some broad hints about its likely policy preferences and, thus, the potential for conflict with the United States.

China is a highly centralized state dominated by a single political party that fuses state and society. Local governors may appear to have substantial authority, but it is clearly delegated and controlled from the center (Landry 2008). In turn, with its special position guaranteed by the Constitution, the party retains a parallel structure to the state and, through its cadre system, permeates all levels of society both channeling issues upward to the center for resolution and ensuring that directives from the center are appropriately implemented at the local level. Factions within the party compete, though programmatic differences appear limited and personal relationships among party elites are more important. Importantly, the party and state stand above the law, not subject to it, and personal connections and influence apparently figure large in political decisions. In an oft-repeated phrase, China is characterized by rule by law but not the rule of law. Finally, after decades of near-totalitarian rule and single party dominance, private authorities able to restrain the state have either been fractured, coopted, or purged from the political system (Yu and Guo 2012). Although new social forces are arising in China and penetrating politics (Saich 2000; Mertha 2009), they remain highly fragmented (Yang 2006). This highly decentralized society leaves a relatively open playing field for the state and its new private-sector allies.

Though significantly liberalized relative to the past, the state and party retain control over the economy through continued government planning and price setting, state-owned enterprises in key sectors, and control over access to scarce finance, access to factors of production, industry setting and the development of new enterprises, and a variety of other economic levers. The fusion of public and private authority in China ensures reciprocal influence between business and the state and relatively harmonious interests between government and private elites (Li, Meng, Wang, and Zhou 2008; Chen and Dickson 2010). Promoting export-led growth since the economic reforms of 1978, China's economy has grown rapidly. Business has profited handsomely, and the state has enjoyed increased legitimacy by its ability to deliver higher standards of living to the average citizen (Laliberte and Lanteigne 2008; Guo 2010). More directly, and reflecting the importance of personal ties in a state-dominated economy, family members of high-ranking party officials have amassed large fortunes either as favored entrepreneurs or as intermediaries between business and the state.

The mutual dependence of public and private elites on export-led growth suggests, at one level, that China will continue to support international economic liberalism. The factions are sometimes described as the elitist faction of officials rising through the party from the more prosperous provinces and the populist faction of officials from the rural interior (Li 2009). For an alternative ordering of the factions, see Zhiyue (2007). On China's "bamboo economy," see *The Economist*, "Entrepreneurship in China: Let a Million Flowers Bloom," March 10, 2011.

For those in the West who see China as more a partner than a competitor in world politics, the expectation is that the vesting of its export industries in the state, and vice versa, will lock China into the present American imperium and liberal international economy. Evidence of this can be found in the tendency of the United States and China to bargain hard but ultimately settle their differences and, more deeply, the possible emergence of an interconnected, transnational global capitalist class of US, European, and Chinese business leaders.

At another level, however, China's statist economy fits poorly with the free and open competition and the rules embedded in the institutions of the American imperium. China's ideal international economy might look a lot like its domestic economy with markets functioning widely but with the permission and in the interests of its political leaders. A Chinese-led international regime would likely not operate under the impersonal rules of the American imperium but under personal ties and to the advantage of China's individual political leaders. In this view, the United States and China might not clash over whether the international economy should be market-based, but would differ significantly on whether markets would be governed by prices or politics. This is less of an ideological distance, perhaps, than that which separated the market-oriented United States and command-oriented Soviet Union at the height of the Cold War, but it is still a substantial distance in preferred rules for the international economy.

Whether or not China chooses to accommodate or challenge the American imperium will depend in large measure on the gains for its leaders as individuals and a group from a liberal market-based international economy versus a state market-based international economy. The challenge, if it occurs, will be rooted in the differing domestic structures of the two twenty-first-century superpowers. Integration into the American imperium is not likely to disrupt China's domestic structure as deeply as World War II and the American occupation did to its postwar allies. China is less likely to change its fundamental institutions than either Germany or Japan. Given the vesting of business in the state, and vice versa, the most likely prospect is for at least a degree of international challenge in the future. Domestic rule conflicts with an international rule of law, and like the United States before it, China will seek to promote its domestic system abroad.

Scholars interested in the future of US–China relations should pay particular attention to the composition of the "winning coalition" in China. Is the party elite composed of those with bases of political support in the most competitive sectors of the economy, or those who rely on the backing of the least competitive sectors? Is the political opposition drawn from the "netizens" in China who favor political and economic transparency or nationalists who regularly engage in anti-foreign protests? To the extent that the winners from globalization win politically, the tensions between the United States and China will be less intense, and to the extent that the losers from globalization triumph politically, these tensions will be greater.

Conclusion

The brightest future for the American imperium is for China's growing middle class to demand a rule of law within China. This is, in part, what the United States and the West more generally hope to achieve in pressing China on human rights and other "internal" political practices. Since such reforms would restrain the state and its high-ranking officials, and reduce their rent-seeking abilities, they are resisted. The United States and others, in turn, are limited in the present. Shirk (2007) argues that China's domestic regime is actually quite fragile, given threats from below from those both empowered by economic prosperity and shut out of the political system. The international balance hangs on the domestic balance between the forces of resistance in China currently vested in

> **The international balance hangs on the domestic balance between the forces of resistance in China currently vested in the state and popular forces of reform calling for greater rule of law.**

the state and popular forces of reform calling for greater rule of law. Without significant private authorities able to help the masses overcome their collective action problems, the vested interests are likely to prevail and the challenge to the American imperium is likely to be serious. What is to be done? Increased trade and investment by the West with China is incentive compatible, and may eventually "tip" the political balance in China in a more liberal direction or at least mitigate the interests now vested in a more politically based system. Confrontation with China will only reinforce those who would seek a Chinese Asian Co-prosperity Sphere. The United States and others should do everything possible to encourage the rule of law and price-led market incentives in China. At the same time, the optimal strategy toward China—no matter its internal fissures—is to maintain the power and resilience of the American imperium, including strengthening relations with other members. Maintaining a strong and open international economy that China wants to be part of—and maintaining a unified front in enforcing the rules of that economy —will maximize leverage for all over China's future and the fate of its possible challenge.

What Wall Street Gets Wrong about China

By Bill Powell
Newsweek Global, August 25, 2015

The number of so-called experts yammering on television about China who know next to nothing about China has reached an all-time high. And for these pseudo-Sinologists, the verdict is in: China, the world's great growth story, is imploding. Its stock market plummeted—down five straight trading days between August 19 and 24—and its real economy is slowing. Because China is the second-largest economy and one of the U.S.'s biggest trading partners, some analysts say Beijing is going to drag it down with them.

Except it's not that simple. And for those of us who work in China as reporters and correspondents—particularly for those like me, who've been here a long time—that reaction has been nothing short of depressing. Apparently, no one reads anything we write.

The immediate cause of the market's volatility was an unexpected "devaluation" of China's currency—the renminbi—on August 10 and 11. For more than a decade, the renminbi had either been stable against the U.S. dollar or appreciated steadily. But when Beijing allowed it to sink by 3 percent over the course of two trading days, it seemed shocking—mainly because of what's going on elsewhere in the world. Two major currencies (the euro and the Japanese yen) and a whole host of minor ones (the Russian ruble, the Brazilian real, etc.) have been sharply devalued over the past couple of years. These devaluations have intensified deflationary pressures in the global economy, because goods and services, in dollar terms, have become less expensive. If China decides to join the beggar-thy-neighbor parade, and further weakens its currency to help its flagging export sector, I would be concerned.

That's how the markets took the news. But it's likely the wrong interpretation. Beijing eventually wants the renminbi to be more like the dollar: a currency that international trade is priced in and that foreign central banks hold as reserves. China also wants the renminbi to be part of the International Monetary Fund's special drawing rights scheme—a supplementary stash of foreign exchange to be used only in extreme circumstances. The IMF declined to admit the renminbi earlier this summer, saying the currency needs to be subject to market forces. At about 6.2 renminbi to the dollar, most economists believed the Chinese currency was slightly overvalued. The 3 percent devaluation signaled that the People's Bank of China

(Beijing's Fed) was going to allow the renminbi to float a bit more. Anything else was a secondary concern.

So despite all the brouhaha, China is not undergoing a Japanese- or European-style devaluation. The government is simply managing an economic transition. Since the government of President Xi Jinping and Prime Minister Li Keqiang came to power in 2012, Beijing has made it clear that the engines of the Chinese economy—investment and exports—need to give way to growth driven by consumption. The Communist Party's platform also stated that "market forces" will be "decisive" going forward. That was a signal that the era of heft loans to state-owned companies to build infrastructure was coming to a close. It also means, as the government acknowledged, annual growth rates were going to come down. The target this year is 7 percent—down significantly from the 10 percent era that lasted more than a decade—and one that Beijing may not even hit.

The transition to a more consumer-led economy will take time, but it is occurring. Consumption accounted for 60 percent of China's gross domestic product (GDP) in the first half of this year. In 2015, the service sector and consumption will be bigger than the manufacturing and construction for the third straight year. Personal income continues to grow at nearly 10 percent annually.

Is this transition bad news? For companies that bet on China growing at a double-digit pace forever, sure. But it's also normal. Economic history shows that when a sizable economy like China's moves from one growth model to another, the shift is rarely painless. This happened to Brazil in the 1960s and Korea and Japan in the 1990s. As Beijing-based economist Michael Pettis writes in his book *The Great Rebalancing*, "The impact…will probably manifest itself in the form of a 'lost' decade or longer for China."

Is that why Chinese equities have crashed? Not so much. China's stock market is a speculative hothouse, and it is not very indicative of where the economy is going. Only 7 percent of the urban population own stocks, and 69 percent of Chinese have less than the equivalent of $15,000 in their accounts, according to Andy Rothman, senior investment strategist at Matthews Asia. So just because its stock market has been cratering, doesn't mean that the Chinese economy—or the American one, for that matter—will go into recession.

To some extent, it makes sense that the American stock market buckled on the news of slower Chinese growth. Corporate leaders, like many equity analysts, tend to fall in love with straight-line analysis, and during the first decade of this century, when it came to China's economy, that straight line was only going up. China was supposed to quickly become the world's largest market for everything, so the U.S. Fortune 500, and everyone else, invested heavily on that assumption. A friend of mine serves on the board of two large U.S. manufacturers, and he says their sales growth in China is 4 to 6 percent this year. The problem is, they had planned for 8 to 10 percent growth. Partly as a result, both companies are now losing money in China—the first time in more than a decade.

But the American market clearly overreacted. On August 24, Apple chief executive Tim Cook took the unusual step of emailing CNBC's Jim Cramer to say that

> **So just because its stock market has been cratering, doesn't mean that the Chinese economy—or the American one, for that matter—will go into recession.**

iPhone sales are growing faster than he had expected in China. Why would that be the case? Because urban consumers have money, and they are still spending. And that's not going to change anytime soon. Investors seemed to finally recognize this when the market rallied on August 26 and 27.

Despite all the doomsday rhetoric on television, China's economic transition will be good for the global economy in the long term. Though Beijing had a reputation for driving growth, its currency manipulation led to big trade surpluses that actually stripped growth from its trading partners. Now that will change. After the close of trading on August 25, the People's Bank of China announced further cuts in interest rates and in its reserves—policy steps it hopes will increase cash in the economy, and thus consumption. As Patrick Chovanec, managing director and chief strategist at Silvercrest Asset Management in New York, puts it: "By propping up consumption in the face of an otherwise wrenching economic adjustment, China can become a source of much-needed demand, and a true growth-driver for the world economy."

China, of course, does have a debt problem; the country's overall debt has surged from an estimated 85 percent of GDP in 2008 to about 280 percent now. That's debt held largely in the hands of state-owned enterprises, the financing arms of local governments and real estate developers. This means that there is virtually no chance the government can use a massive credit jolt to jumpstart the economy. The question is whether they can avoid an unexpected debt crisis—a big bank run or large defaults in the shadow banking sector. Neither is beyond the realm of possibility. But if China's growth slows over time, and debt issuance grows ever more slowly, the country's troublesome debt-to-GDP ratio can begin to shrink.

In other words, the boom is over, but Beijing isn't burning. Slower growth may be exactly what China and the world needs.

Cyber-Espionage Nightmare

By David Talbot

MIT Technology Review, July 2015

On a wall facing dozens of cubicles at the FBI office in Pittsburgh, five guys from Shanghai stare from "Wanted" posters. Wang Dong, Sun Kailiang, Wen Xinyu, Huang Zhenyu, and Gu Chunhui are, according to a federal indictment unsealed last year, agents of China's People's Liberation Army Unit 61398, who hacked into networks at American companies—U.S. Steel, Alcoa, Allegheny Technologies (ATI), Westinghouse—plus the biggest industrial labor union in North America, United Steelworkers, and the U.S. subsidiary of SolarWorld, a German solar-panel maker. Over several years, prosecutors say, the agents stole thousands of e-mails about business strategy, documents about unfair-trade cases some of the U.S. companies had filed against China, and even piping designs for nuclear power plants—all allegedly to benefit Chinese companies.

It is the first case the United States has brought against the perpetrators of alleged state-sponsored cyber-espionage, and it has revealed computer-security holes that companies rarely acknowledge in public. Although the attackers apparently routed their activities through innocent people's computers and made other efforts to mask themselves, prosecutors traced the intrusions to a 12-story building in Shanghai and Alex Williamson, who outed individual intelligence agents. There is little chance that arrests will be made, since the United States has no extradition agreements with China, but the U.S. government apparently hopes that naming actual agents—and demonstrating that tracing attacks is possible—will embarrass China and put other nations on notice, inhibiting future economic espionage.

That may be unrealistic. Security companies say such activity is continuing, and China calls the accusations "purely ungrounded and absurd." But there's another lesson from the indictment: businesses are now unlikely to keep valuable information secure online. Whatever steps they are taking are not keeping pace with the threats. "Clearly the situation has gotten worse, not better," says Virgil Gligor, who co-directs Carnegie Mellon University's computer security research center, known as CyLab. "We made access to services and databases and connectivity so convenient that it is also convenient for our adversaries." Once companies accept that, Gligor says, the most obvious response is a drastic one: unplug.

Fracking and Hacking

Sitting at a small conference table in his office in the federal courthouse in Pittsburgh, David Hickton, the United States attorney for western Pennsylvania, opened a plastic container he'd brought from home and removed and peeled a hardboiled egg for lunch. Although we were discussing an investigation involving global players and opaque technologies, the homey feel of our meeting was apt: the case had many roots in close-knit business and political circles in Pittsburgh. Hickton showed me a framed photo on a shelf. In the picture, he and a friend named John Surma are standing next to their sons, the boys wearing hockey uniforms, fresh from the ice. Both fathers had attended Penn State. As Hickton rose in the prosecutorial ranks, Surma rose in the corporate world, becoming CEO of U.S. Steel. When Hickton became the top federal prosecutor in the area in 2010, one of his meet-and-greet breakfasts was with Surma and Leo Girard, the boss of United Steelworkers, which represents 1.2 million current or retired workers in several industries. "I was asking them in a completely unrelated matter to serve on a youth crime prevention council," Hickton recalls. "They said, 'Can we talk to you about something else?'"

At the time, the American fracking boom was in full swing, with ultra-low interest rates that had been set to stimulate the economy also lubricating the business of extracting previously hard-to-reach natural gas and oil. U.S. Steel had a flourishing business selling pipes specially designed for the extraction process. Among other traits, the pipes have no vertical seams, so they will hold up as they're rammed thousands of feet into the earth and yet bend to convey oil and gas without breaking.

But U.S. Steel also noticed two unsettling developments. First, Chinese state-owned companies were exporting lots of similar pipe into the United States at low prices. So U.S. Steel filed complaints with the U.S. Department of Commerce and the U.S. International Trade Commission, accusing China of subsidizing its industries; the resulting cases ultimately led to sanctions against China. Second, both the company and the union were aware that suspicious e-mails had come in. But it wasn't clear who was behind them or whether any damage was occurring. "There was a general awareness of intrusions, but not 'when, where, how' and the scope," Hickton says.

The Online Spy's Toolkit
Malware on your computer (or someone elses) can give snoops a place to hide.

Hackers

Hop point

Hop points are ordinary computers that can be remotely controlled without their owners' knowledge.

Company computer infected with malware

The e-mails were cleverly designed. They purported to be from colleagues or board members, with subject lines relating to meeting agendas or market re-search, but they delivered malware by means of attachments or links. For example, the indictment says, on February 8, 2010—two weeks before a preliminary ruling from the Commerce Department—the hackers sent an e-mail to several U.S. Steel employees. It seemed to be from the CEO but included a link to a website that held malware. A few employees clicked it, and their computers were soon infected. The result: the hackers stole host names for 1,700 servers that controlled access to the company's facilities and networks. The indictment says Wang then tried to exploit that access, but it doesn't specify what information was exposed.

> **A groundbreaking online-spying case unearths details that companies wish you didn't know about how vital information slips away from them.**

Debbie Shon, U.S. Steel's vice president for trade, told me that the information included valuable business intelligence. "It wasn't high-tech designs," she says. "It was the equally important stuff—the business strategies, the pricing, the production amounts, and the timing and content of any trade complaints that U.S. Steel, as one of the biggest companies in this area, might be exploring."

The indictment details several similar attacks. Between 2007 and 2013, Westinghouse was negotiating the details of a contract with a Chinese company to build four nuclear reactors. From 2010 to 2012, one of the defendants allegedly stole at least 1.4 gigabytes of data—roughly 700,000 pages of e-mail and attachments—from Westinghouse's computers. The files included piping designs and communications in which Westinghouse disclosed worries about Chinese competition. At ATI, the hackers allegedly stole the passwords of 7,000 employees while the company was in a trade dispute focused on its sales to China. At Alcoa, prosecutors allege, the hackers stole 2,900 e-mails with more than 860 attachments around the time the company was negotiating deals with Chinese businesses. (Alcoa, Westinghouse, and ATI all declined to comment for this story.) And in 2012, after the steelworkers' union started speaking out against Chinese industrial policies, Wen stole e-mails containing discussions among union leaders, the indictment says.

Meanwhile, SolarWorld had brought trade cases accusing Chinese companies of selling solar panels below cost, decimating their rivals. One day in 2012, a phone rang at its offices in Camarillo, California. It was the FBI calling, saying that agents had discovered e-mails stolen from the company, says Ben Santarris, its U.S. spokesman. In a sign of just how bad cybersecurity is, "there was no inkling this was going on until we got the phone call," he says. Only when the indictment was unsealed in May 2014 did the company learn the full scope of the alleged theft. "There was access to trade-case strategy, company financials, costs, profit-and-loss statements, technology road maps, R&D, and so on," Santarris says. Ultimately the company won its cases, securing duties on imports of solar equipment from China. During the trade dispute, "we were observing very tight controls over who gets to see what information," he says. "At the time we were doing that, according to the FBI, the Chinese military was coming in the back door."

Take It Down

The failure of the companies' supposed security technologies was stupefying. Lance Wyatt, the IT director for the steelworkers' union, thought he ran a tight ship. An IT audit in 2010 had found no major deficiencies. His e-mail server screened all incoming messages for attachments that contained executable code. He had the latest antivirus software. His network checked IP addresses to avoid sites that contained malware. Yet Wyatt and the FBI eventually found infected computers, one of them used by the union's travel manager. "None of those machines were on our radar as being infected or suspect," he says.

According to the indictment, the hackers had various means of disguise. For one thing, they allegedly sent malicious e-mail into companies and the union from hop points—intermediate computers, including one in Kansas, that were under their control. Second, they skillfully manipulated the Internet's system for naming computer addresses. The hackers set up domain names such as "arrowservice.net" and "purpledaily.com" and programmed malware on the corporate victim computers to contact them. Then the spies could continually change the computer addresses to which the domain names connected. When it was daytime in Shanghai and nighttime in Pittsburgh, the indictment says, they'd set a domain name to connect to hop-point computers and conduct espionage. When the Shanghai workday was done, the hackers would set the address to connect to innocuous sites such as Yahoo pages.

> **Prosecutors say they traced computer break-ins to these agents in Shanghai, who allegedly used such online nicknames as UglyGorilla.**

It's not a surprise that such systems are relatively easy to co-opt for nefarious purposes. Ideas for making the Internet more secure have been around for decades, and academic and government labs have churned out interesting proposals. Yet very few of these ideas have been implemented; they require broad-based adoption and possibly trade-offs in network performance. "You don't hear about rebuilding the Internet anymore," says Greg Shannon, chief scientist at the CERT division of Carnegie Mellon's Software Engineering Institute.

What's a company to do? Wyatt tightened things at United Steelworkers; among other things, he now gives fewer employees so-called administrative privileges to their computers, and he searches the network for the telltale signs of communications by malware. But none of this would have prevented the intrusions. Wyatt says it "might have slowed them down."

The best option, then, could be to get sensitive data off the Internet entirely. There are downsides to that: if e-mail is not used as freely, or a database is offline, keeping up with the latest versions of reports or other data could be more time-consuming. But as Gligor says: "We must pay the cost of security, which is inconvenience. We need to add a little inconvenience for us to make things much harder for the remote attacker. The way to do that is to—how should I put it?—occasionally go offline."

After all, more attacks like the ones in Pittsburgh are still occurring. "This indictment," Hickton says, "does not represent the full number of hackers, full number of victims, or full number of defendants."

Heads Together on the China-U.S. Bilateral Investment Treaty

By Zhang Wenzong
China Today, June 2015

Progress on the U.S.-China Bilateral Investment Treaty (BIT) is expected to be a main focus of public attention at the seventh round of the China-U.S. Strategy & Economic Dialogue (S&ED) this month in the United States. The annual S&ED agenda will likely include standard issues such as renminbi exchange rates, IMF quotas, actualizing governance structure reforms, and the United States' stance on the Asian Infrastructure Investment Bank (AIIB). The sixth round of the Dialogue last year saw completion of the agreement's text on core provisions, and of negotiations on key issues, so clearing the way for talks on the negative list. The two countries' decision-makers appear keen to speed things up, and news releases imply that reaching agreement is but a matter of time. Available information on the upcoming S&ED, the future of the BIT and its impact on China-U.S. relations, and the investment structure of international trade and economy, however, warrants close attention.

Negotiations on Track

As a bilateral treaty, the aim of the BIT is to encourage citizens of both countries to invest in one another and to promote and protect such investment. Its content encompasses protection, investment treatment, expropriation and compensation, currency exchange, and dispute resolution. Both China and the United States have signed BITs with other countries. As the top two world economies, they have, under a deep political and economic background, been doing their utmost to advance negotiations. Since the financial crisis of 2008, the international economy has gone through significant adjustment. New features are apparent in the economic situation and relations between China and the United States, and their domestic and foreign policies. The start and accomplishment of the BIT now seems to be in sight.

First of all, the treaty addresses both China and the United States' need for economic reform. Following profound changes in demographic structure, production factor prices, and the international economic situation, the Chinese economy has bid farewell to its golden period of two-digit growth and entered a "new normal" of slower growth and an adjusted development mode. Releasing further reform dividends and promoting a higher-level of opening-up has become an important consensus of the new-generation Chinese leadership. This became evident during the Third Plenary Session of the 18th Central Committee of the Communist Party of China, when it was elevated to a national strategy. Having been hit hard by the financial crisis, the United States has started to reflect on its development mode. While strengthening its virtual economy management, the Obama administration must also revitalize the manufacturing industry in an all-out effort to reinvigorate the real economy. It can thus improve people's well-being and consolidate its world "leading status." Both sides require healthier, more sustainable development and better, safer investment to propel their reforms. The changes in the two countries' economic structure and economic policies constitute the foundation for signing the bilateral investment treaty.

The treaty also adapts to changes in China-U.S. economic relations. The global economy downturn had a grim effect on China's exports, which have picked up little since the American economy recovered. The excessive production capacity of some of China's commodities, and U.S. protectionism towards China are significant factors in the slow growth of China's exports to the United States.

China's investment in the United States, however, has grown rapidly. Ministry of Commerce statistics show that it rose from US $1.88 billion in 2007 to US $9.3 billion in 2012. Meanwhile China's direct investment in the United States reached US $8.023 billion in 2013, and the compound annual growth rate grew to 41.54 percent from 2009 to 2013, ranking first worldwide, according to U.S. Department of Commerce statistics. The U.S. Rhodium Group's long-term follow-up study of Chinese investment shows that Chinese enterprises' investment in the United States broke the US $10 million barrier in 2014, when it hit US $12 billion. The "going global" strategy of Chinese enterprises and capital tallies with the Obama administration's "choose the U.S" policy of inviting outside investment. This has had profound impact on China-U.S. trade and investment relations. It is interesting to note that, due to multiple factors, the trend of U.S. direct investment in China in recent years appears to be that of stagnation or even decline. Maintaining its attraction for Western capital, including from the U.S., through reform and opening-up is part of China's efforts to promote the bilateral investment treaty.

The treaty also offers a way of managing the two countries' strategic relations. Since 2010, the U.S. has been promoting the Trans-Pacific Partnership Agreement (TPP) and Transatlantic Trade and Investment Partnership (TTIP). Both are efforts to reverse the negative effects of the financial crisis and globalization and to reinvent international trade and investment rules to impose higher standards more in line with American interests. China, which is excluded, seems to be facing a challenge similar to that of 2001 when it sought to join the WTO. Under the backdrop of intensified Sino-U.S. strategic competition, growing risks of military confrontation and mounting economic and trade frictions, decision-makers in both countries have proved their leadership skills by controlling bilateral relations. To China, the benefits of proactively promoting Regional Comprehensive Economic Partnership (RCEP) and Sino-EU and Sino-U.S. bilateral investment treaty negotiations are twofold: both are (1) conducive to strengthening its economic strength and influence and (2) to maintaining the role of trade and economy in stabilizing the bilateral relations. They also contribute to building new major country relations. The combination of multiple subjective and objective factors thus places the item, "forming a unified management standard for foreign capital entering the other country" firmly on the agenda.

Coexistent Opportunities and Challenges

Negotiations are mainly to do with investment market access, transparency, state-owned enterprises, security interests, labor protection, and environmental standards. China has long operated the examination and approval system of managing foreign capital whereby it awards post-establishment national treatment. Since the strategic deployment of the reform agreed at the Third Plenary Session of the 18th Central Committee of the Communist Party of China, however, China has adopted the principle of "pre-establishment national treatment plus negative list" to push forward relevant negotiations with the United States.

This shows that China accepts the management standards set by the United States, and also that China is "promoting reform through opening-up." Pre-establishment national treatment and negative list signifies that foreign investment projects will switch from the approval system to the filing system. This will simplify examination and approval procedures for foreign investment into China, and make the admission of foreign capital more transparent and efficient. By streamlining administration and delegating power to lower levels China expects to promote its reform of domestic capital management on the same basis as reforms to the foreign capital management system. It will thus eventually "let the market play the decisive role in resource allocation," and create an upgraded version of the Chinese economy.

After the establishment of the Shanghai Free Trade Zone in August 2013, the State Council approved in April 2015 the establishment of three more pilot free trade zones in Guangdong, Tianjin, and Fujian. This was under the stipulation that all four free trade zones would adopt the management mode of pre-establishment national treatment plus negative list. Like the special economic zones of the 1980s, these pilot free trade zones will undoubtedly play an experimental role in the new round of reforms. When the conditions are suitable and the time is right, the China-U.S. Bilateral Investment Treaty, like the Permanent Normal Trade Relations (PNTR), will act as a ticket and passport for China to further integrate into the world economy and access high-standard FTA rules and practice.

The considerable differences between the two countries' political and economic systems, extent of development, degree of market openness, and enterprise competitiveness make the Sino-U.S. BIT negotiations an opportunity to "use the exterior to promote the domestic." They might also affect the economic and institutional foundation of the China-U.S. power game. As it took six years—from 2008 to 2014—for China and the United States to reach agreement on the core articles and main issues of the BIT text, however, negotiations are obviously not easy.

During these negotiations both sides must maximize benefits and minimize risks and losses. The BIT will eventually hit a new balance according to the contrasts between national strength and price demand. It can then promote trade and investment and protect the economic and social security of either host country. Negotiation is a process of resolving differences and reaching a compromise, and hence entails many focuses. Several items merit attention. Although China is committed to the reform of state-owned enterprises, it upholds the principal status of public ownership and the leading role of the state-owned economy. It will not, therefore, unconditionally embrace the U.S. principle of "competitive neutrality" with regard to state-owned enterprises.

As to the high U.S. labor and environment standards, to avoid loss of competitive power China will insist on appropriate arrangements geared to Chinese conditions. Whether or not the BIT can resolve misgivings that exist in the two countries is vital. For instance, there are worries in Chinese academic circles about transnational companies' monopoly of China's daily chemical industry and soft drinks industry. Will the BIT aggravate this trend? The U.S. Foreign Investment Review Board's rejection of Sany Heavy Industry and Huawei's Greenfield investment and merger and acquisition project applications makes clear that the United States is sensitive to and suspicious of China's investment.

China and the United States have now compiled negative lists and are prepared to exchange them. Frequent discussions and revisions of these lists will undoubtedly ensue. Both sides will haggle over such items as the scope of prohibited or restricted fields and industries, enhanced transparency of special management measures, rationality of relevant state security examination procedures, and even adjustments of the proportion of certain industries' foreign equity.

The international trade negotiation process is a two level game that involves both countries' domestic interest groups as well as negotiation teams. The China-U.S. BIT may, like negotiations on China's PNTR, also trigger changes in domestic interest patterns, and related effects cannot be ignored. Decision-makers face the problems of whether or not the U.S. administrative department can acquire fast-track authority from Congress, whether or not changes in the political ecology will influence the future of the BIT, and whether or not TTP and TTIP negotiations will affect the China-U.S. BIT negotiations.

> **The Chinese leadership has also expressed confidence in preventing risks through improvements to the national security review system, and by perfecting the during-process and after-event supervision.**

Even when negotiations are concluded and the agreement comes into force, a number of contingency questions will still remain. For instance, taking into account the uneven economic development between various provinces, will a transitional period in which to apply the accumulated pilot FTA experience of foreign capital management be necessary? Will there be any impediments to reducing the examination and approval authority of a dozen or more government departments, including the Ministry of Commerce, the National Development and Reform Commission, China Banking Regulatory Commission, and China Insurance Regulatory Commission, so breaking the interests of these sectors and the inertia of their thinking? The United States needs funds from all over the world to support its economic recovery and prosperity. Bearing in mind the particularity of China-U.S. relations, however, when China's capital enters the U.S.'s fields of information and communications technology, energy, foodstuffs, and real estate, and participates in mergers and acquisitions of American enterprises, will there be any recurrence of adverse reactions from conservative politicians and dissatisfaction among the populace? How best to plan, control the risks, promote the beneficial and abolish the harmful will test the wisdom of both countries' policy-makers.

China's Positive Efforts

No matter the risks and challenges, China's practical measures provide the answers. Premier Li Keqiang told visiting U.S. Secretary of Commerce Penny Pritzker on April 13 that the Chinese government will expand the opening up of the service and general manufacturing industries and halve the restraints on foreign investment. The State Council stipulated in its recently documented approval to build three pilot free trade zones that all four free trade zones will adopt the new negative list of 122 items with special management measures—60 plus items fewer than the first Shanghai Free Trade Zone list released in 2013.

Meanwhile, the Chinese leadership has also expressed confidence in preventing risks through improvements to the national security review system, and by perfecting the during-process and after-event supervision. While seizing the opportunities of a new round of foreign investment industry layouts and coping with the new risks attendant upon foreign investments entering the country, the Chinese government must also provide political support and institutional guarantees for Chinese nationals and legal persons investing overseas. In 2014, China's outbound investment amounted to US $140 billion, surpassing inbound investment by US $20 billion. China thus became a net capital exporting country, according to the China Two-way Investment Development Report 2014. The USA Asia Society predicts that by the year 2020, China's direct investment throughout the world will surpass US $1 trillion, and that a great proportion of it will go to developed countries such as the United States. Creating for Chinese entrepreneurs an open, just and transparent competitive market overseas, and helping them safeguard their legitimate rights and interests when disputes arise is a new embodiment of governing for the people.

2
The Environment, Sustainable Energy, and Natural Resources

An oil truck runs past wind turbines at the Dafancheng Wind Power Plant, the largest of its kind in Asia, on September 2, 2007 in Dafancheng of Xinjiang Uygur Autonomous Region, China.

Environmental Conflict and Cooperation

At over 9.5 million kilometers, China is one of the world's most environmentally diverse nations. From arid deserts to frozen tundra, the nation's biomes and microenvironments once supported a dizzying diversity of wildlife and provided sufficient natural resources to fuel one of the longest continuous civilizations on the planet. Mainland China borders the East China Sea, the Yellow Sea and the South China Sea and, with a long history of aquaculture and fishing, exerts tremendous environmental impact on surrounding oceanic environments. The western part of China contains vast deserts that have been growing for centuries, gradually transforming the nation's plains and agricultural valleys into barren sand dunes. In the twenty-first century, China has become one of the world's most polluted environments. The people and remaining wildlife in China face severe air, water, and soil pollution levels that pose a constant threat to China's human population and are gradually dwindling the nation's complement of wildlife as well.

World Powers and Global Polluters

China and the United States have much in common when it comes to environmental threats. While the United States has not yet achieved the levels of air and water pollution found in China, the United States ranks 2nd (behind China) in the world in terms of carbon emissions. China and the United States are therefore the two nations that contribute most to climate change and global warming.[1] In addition, as the United States and China rank as the world's 1st and 2nd largest economies, respectively, both nations exert tremendous economic influence over the rest of the world and the environmental policies enacted by both nations—because of size and economic influence—have potentially global impact. While China and the United States clash on economic and social issues, the two nations have taken steps towards making agreements on key environmental initiatives. U.S.-based environmental agencies are active in China and joint scientific/ecological studies have allowed both nations to share data and cooperate on strategies to combat environmental degradation.

Climate Change

Climate change is one of the most controversial political/environmental issues of the twenty-first century. Despite a passionate lobby arguing against human-mediated climate change, scientific analysis has clearly demonstrated that climate change is occurring and the governments of both China and the United States have taken the official position that climate change is related, directly, to human activity. Specifically, the burning of fossil fuels and production of carbon emissions has been directly linked to global warming. As of 2013, China produced 2.1 billion tons of carbon dioxide emissions, while the United States produced 1.4 billion tons, making China and the United States the world's leading producers of carbon emissions.[2]

In 2013, Chinese and U.S. politicians came together to create a new U.S.-China Working Group on Climate Change, which was charged with creating legislative recommendations on reducing emissions from coal, heavy vehicles, and automobiles and of increasing focus on energy efficiency and the use of renewable or green energy in cities and industry.[3] In a series of closed negotiations in 2014, 2015, and 2016, Presidents Barack Obama and Xi Jinping discussed ways that both nations could slow carbon emissions and invest in sustainable technology and energy. The first public announcement from these meetings, released in November of 2014, included specific environmental goals for both nations. President Obama vowed that the United States would reduce carbon emissions from 26 to 28 percent by 2025, while President Xi pledged that China will utilize green energy for 20 percent of the nation's energy needs and will make efforts to reach peak carbon pollution levels by 2030.[4] A year later, in a second joint announcement, both governments pledged to work together to create $100 billion in funding to help developing nations reduce carbon emissions and invest in sustainable energy.[5]

The 2015 United Nations Climate Change Conference (COP 21) was held in Paris, France in November and December of 2015. The ultimate goal of the conference was to create international agreements towards the goal of limiting the extent of global warming to 2 degrees Celsius above pre-industrial levels and to fully eradicate human-created greenhouse emissions during the second half of the twenty-first century. These goals, and the agreements made to achieve them (known as the Paris Agreement), become law if ratified by at least 55 nations that together create 55 percent or more of the nation's greenhouse emissions. In March of 2016, China and the United States released a joint announcement that both nations would ratify the Paris Agreements on April 22, 2015. If the Paris Agreement is ratified by the required 55 nations, countries that violate the agreement terms could be subject to United Nations sanctions and penalties.[6]

China's environmental goals between 2015 and 2030 are far more ambitious than the relatively modest goals of the United States during the same period. To achieve the goal, China will have to cut current carbon pollution levels by 20 billion tons between 2015 and 2030. However, China's pollution problem has reached epidemic levels, especially in the nation's largest cities such as Beijing, Shenyang, and Shanghai where urban pollution is visible from space. Though the nation is the world's largest polluter, China has also invested more in green energy than any other nation since 2010.[7] Chinese public opinion polls indicate that a majority of the Chinese population see pollution as among the nation's top problems and this shift in public opinion (in the 2000s and 2010s) is motivating more aggressive legislation on the issue.[8]

Oceanic Conservation

China and the United States also have many shared interests in the arena of oceanic conservation. Overfishing depletes food supplies in oceanic environments, while water and air pollution pollute oceans, reduce planktonic growth, and collectively threaten entire marine food chains. According to some estimates, China will consume 38 percent of the global seafood harvest by 2030, and thus the nation has a vested interest, and, some argue an international responsibility, to invest in marine conservation. The current patterns of overfishing and reduction in fish stocks will affect more than 2 billion people globally. Currently, Asian nations operate nearly 3 million of the world's 4 million fishing vessels, with China maintaining the largest commercial fishing fleet in the world. China claims more than one-third of all fish harvested annually, while the United States ranks third in terms of fish and seafood consumption. According to 2013 estimates, commercial fishing was one of China's largest industries, employing an estimated 14.4 million people.[9]

In an effort to protect fishing industries, both the United States and China have been participants in an emerging form of development known as the "Blue Economy," in which the government invests in the development of oceanic resources, helping to create jobs and protect marine industries, while attempting to control pollution in an effort to conserve marine resources. Between 2006 and 2010, China created 33 million jobs through the nation's Blue Economy initiatives, though environmental studies indicate that China's oceanic industry expansion is hastening the depletion of fish stocks and increasing pollution. The United States, which has the largest economic fishing area in the world, has dedicated significantly more attention to environmental protection than China, though critics argue that the United States remains one of the world's leading agents of oceanic degradation.[10]

China's demand for fishing territory plays a role in the nation's recent territorial expansion into the South China Sea. China has recently invested in building a series of artificial islands in the Spratly Island Chain, dredging the ocean floor surrounding the region's coral reef habitat. Conservationists around the world objected to China's activities in the region, arguing that the construction of the artificial islands will damage the fragile coral reef habitat in the area. In addition, expanding fishing operations in the region are likely to further deplete already limited fish stocks.[11]

Marine conservation was one of the issues discussed between President Obama and President Xi, during a set of closed 2015 meetings. Obama and Xi pledged to work together towards the establishment of a Marine Protected Area (MPA) in Antarctica's Ross Sea and agreed to work together on the development of new ocean acidification monitoring methods. Obama and Xi also agreed to create a new urban conservation program in the coastal cities of San Francisco, New York, Xiamen, and Weihai, to cooperate on creating methods for reducing the flow of solid waste and pollution from urban coastal environments.[12]

Environmental Priorities

Environmental conservation projects like the International Program on the State of the Ocean and the Society for Conservation Biology have determined that Earth's environment is reaching a critical state, with global warming, human-generated pollution, and loss of species proceeding at an alarming rate. Despite increasing their conservation efforts, environmental organizations warn that current conservation policies are insufficient to slow the current progress of environmental degradation. Media reports indicate the environmental issues have become a top priority for the Chinese population since 2010, and environmental conservation consistently ranks among the top ten social issues for American citizens as well. As the global environment is, by its nature, a collective concern for all humanity, combating these many pressing issues, despite their complexity, can also provide the impetus for new dialogue and international cooperation.

Micah L. Issitt

Recommended Readings

"China's Environmental Crisis." *CFR*. Council on Foreign Relations. Jan 18 2016. Web. 6 Apr 2016.

Conathan, Michael and Scott Moore. "Developing a Blue Economy in China and the United States." *American Progress*. Center for American Progress. May 2015. Pdf. 6 Apr 2016.

"FACT SHEET: President Xi Jinping's State Visit to the United States." *Whitehouse*. Office of the Press Secretary. Sep 25 2015. Web. 6 Apr 2016.

Johnson, William. "Everything You Need to Know About the South China Sea Conflict—In Under Five Minutes." *Reuters*. Thompson Reuters. Jun 9 2015. Web. 6 Apr 2016.

Nuccitelli, Dana. "Fact Check: China Pledged Bigger Climate Action than the USA; Republican Leaders Wrong." *The Guardian*. Guardian News and Media Limited. Nov 14 2014. Web. 6 Apr 2016.

Sedghi, Ami. "China v the US: How the Superpowers Compare." *The Guardian*. Guardian News and Media Limited. Jun 7 2013. Web. 3 Apr 2016.

"The East in Grey." *The Economist*. Economist Newspaper Limited. Aug 10 2013. Web. 6 Apr 2016.

"U.S.-China Climate Change Working Group Fact Sheet." *U.S. Department of State*. Office of the Spokesperson. Jul 10 2013. Web. 4 Apr 2016.

"U.S.-China Joint Announcement on Climate Change." *White House*. Office of the Press Secretary. Nov 11 2014. Web. 5 Apr 2016.

"U.S.-China Joint Presidential Statement on Climate Change." *Whitehouse*. Office of the Press Secretary. Sep 25 2015. Web. 6 Apr 2016.

"U.S.-China Joint Presidential Statement on Climate Change." *Whitehouse*. Office of the Press Secretary. Mar 31 2016. Web. 7 Apr 2016.

Zhang Hongzhou. "China's Evolving Fishing Industry: Implications for Regional and Global Maritime Security." *RSIS*. S. Rajaratnam School of International Studies Singapore. Aug 16 2012. Web. 6 Apr 2016.

Notes

1. "China's Environmental Crisis." *CFR*.

2. Sedghi, "China v the US: How the Superpowers Compare."

3. "U.S.-China Climate Change Working Group Fact Sheet."

4. "U.S.-China Joint Announcement on Climate Change," Nov 11 2014.

5. "U.S.-China Joint Presidential Statement on Climate Change," Sep 25 2015.

6. "U.S.-China Joint Presidential Statement on Climate Change," Mar 31 2016.

7. "The East in Grey," *The Economist*.

8. Nuccitelli, "Fact Check: China Pledged Bigger Climate Action than the USA; Republican Leaders Wrong."

9. Zhang, "China's Evolving Fishing Industry: Implications for Regional and Global Maritime Security."

10. Conathan and Moore, "Developing a Blue Economy in China and the United States."

11. Johnson, "Everything You Need to Know About the South China Sea Conflict—In Under Five Minutes."

12. "Fact Sheet: President Xi Jinping's State Visit to the United States," Sep 25 2015.

China's Environmental Crisis

By Eleanor Albert and Beina Xu
Council on Foreign Relations, January 18, 2016

China's environmental crisis is one of the most pressing challenges to emerge from the country's rapid industrialization. Its economic rise, in which GDP grew on average 10 percent each year for more than a decade, has come at the expense of its environment and public health. China is the world's largest source of carbon emissions, and the air quality of many of its major cities fails to meet international health standards. Life expectancy north of the Huai River is 5.5 years lower than in the south due to air pollution (life expectancy in China is 75.3 according to 2013 UN figures). Severe water contamination and scarcity have compounded land deterioration. Environmental degradation threatens to undermine the country's growth and exhausts public patience with the pace of reform. It has also bruised China's international standing and endangered domestic stability as the ruling party faces increasing scrutiny and public discontent. More recently, amid waning economic growth, leaders in Beijing appear more determined to institute changes to stem further degradation.

A History of Pollution

While China's economic boom has greatly accelerated the devastation of its land and resources, the roots of its environmental problem stretch back centuries. Dynastic leaders who consolidated territory and developed China's economy exploited natural resources in ways that contributed to famines and natural disasters, writes the Council on Foreign Relations' (CFR's) Elizabeth C. Economy in *The River Runs Black: The Environmental Challenge to China's Future*. "China's current environmental situation is the result not only of policy choices made today but also of attitudes, approaches, and institutions that have evolved over centuries," Economy writes.

It wasn't until the 1972 United Nations Conference on the Human Environment that China began to develop environmental institutions. It dispatched a delegation to the conference in Stockholm, but by then the country's environment was already in dire straits.

Economic reforms in the late 1970s that encouraged development in rural industries further exacerbated the problem.

Chinese leader Deng Xiaoping implemented a series of reforms that diffused authority to the provinces, creating a proliferation of township and village enterprises (TVEs). By 1997, TVEs generated almost a third of national GDP, though TVEs have since declined in relative importance to the Chinese economy. But local governments were difficult to monitor and seldom upheld environmental standards. Today, with a transitioning Chinese economy fueled by large state-owned enterprises, environmental policies remain difficult to enforce at the local level, where officials often prioritize hitting economic targets over environmental concerns. Despite the government's stated goals, actual change to environmental policies and effective implementation will require revisiting state-society and state-market relations and China's bureaucratic power structure, writes CFR's Yanzhong Huang.

China's modernization has lifted hundreds of millions out of poverty and created a booming middle class. In some ways, the country's trajectory of industrialization is not unlike those of other modernizing nations, such as the UK in the early nineteenth century. But experts say China's environmental footprint is far greater than that of any other single country.

How Bad Is It?

China is the world's largest emitter of greenhouse gases, having overtaken the United States in 2007, and was responsible for 27 percent of global emissions in 2014.

The country's energy consumption has ballooned, with reports from late 2015 implying that it consumed up to 17 percent more coal than previously reported. In January 2013, Beijing experienced a prolonged bout of smog so severe that citizens dubbed it an "airpocalypse"; the concentration of hazardous particles was forty times the level deemed safe by the World Health Organization (WHO). In December 2015, Beijing issued red alerts for severe pollution—the first since the emergency alert system was established. The municipal government closed schools, limited road traffic, halted outdoor construction, and paused factory manufacturing. At least 80 percent of China's 367 cities with real-time air quality monitoring failed to meet national small-particle pollution standards during the first three quarters of 2015, according to a Greenpeace East Asia report. In December 2015, the Asian Development Bank approved a $300 million loan to help China address the capital region's choking smog.

Coal is largely to blame for the degradation of air quality. China is the world's largest coal producer and accounts for about half of global consumption. Mostly burned in the north, coal provides around two-thirds of China's energy mix, however demand for it appears to be declining. China's National Energy Agency claimed that coal use dropped to 64.2 percent of the mix in 2014, down almost two percent from 2012. This drop in coal demand also comes as China's economy is slowing, with its central bank forecasting that annual growth will only expand by 6.8 percent in 2016, down from 6.9 percent a year earlier. Still, doubts linger of China's commitment to wean itself from coal. In 2015, China's coal power plant capacity increased by 55 percent in the first six months, 155 new coal-fired plants were approved, and China admitted that it had underreported its annual coal consumption since 2000.

There were a record 17 million new cars on the road in 2014, further contributing to China's high emissions. Car ownership was up to 154 million, according to China's Ministry of Public Security, with compared to roughly 27 million in 2004, according to China's National Bureau of Statistics. Another trend compounding air problems has been the country's staggering pace of urbanization, a national

> **"China's current environmental situation is the result not only of policy choices made today but also of attitudes, approaches, and institutions that have evolved over centuries."—Elizabeth C. Economy, Council on Foreign Relations**

priority. The government aims to have more than 60 percent of the Chinese population living in cities by 2020, up from 36 percent in 2000 (53.7 percent of the population in 2015 lived in urban areas). Rapid urbanization increases energy demands to power new manufacturing and industrial centers.

Experts also cite water depletion and pollution as among the country's biggest environmental challenges. China is home to 20 percent of the world's population but only 7 percent (PDF) of its fresh water sources. Overuse and contamination have produced severe shortages, with nearly 70 percent of the country's water supplies dedicated to agriculture and 20 percent of supplies used in the coal industry, according to Choke Point: China, an environmental NGO initiative. Approximately two-thirds of China's roughly 660 cities suffer from water shortages. Former Chinese premier Wen Jiabao has said that water shortages challenge "the very survival of the Chinese nation."

Industry along China's major water sources has polluted water supplies: in 2014, groundwater supplies in more than 60 percent of major cities were categorized as "bad to very bad" and more than a quarter of China's key rivers are "unfit for human contact." And lack of waste removal and proper processing has exacerbated problems. Combined with negligent farming practices, overgrazing, and the effects of climate change, the water crisis has turned much of China's arable land into desert. About 1.05 million square miles of China's landmass are undergoing desertification, affecting more than 400 million people, according to the deputy head of China's State Forestry Administration. Water scarcity, pollution, and desertification are reducing China's ability to sustain its industrial output and produce food and drinkable water for its large population.

Cost of Environmental Damage

Environmental depredations pose a serious threat to China's economic growth, costing the country roughly 3 to 10 percent of its gross national income, according to various estimates. China's Ministry of Environmental Protection calculates estimates the cost of pollution at around 1.5 trillion RMB ($227 billion), or roughly 3.5 percent of GDP, according to 2010 figures. Due to the sensitivity of the topic, the ministry only releases such figures intermittently.

Data on the toll of China's pollution on public health paint a devastating picture. Air pollution contributes to an estimated 1.2 million premature deaths in China annually. Epidemiological studies conducted since the 1980s in northern China suggest that poor air quality in Chinese cities causes significant health complications, including respiratory, cardiovascular, and cerebrovascular diseases. Pollution has also been linked to the proliferation of acute and chronic diseases; estimates suggest that around 11 percent of digestive-system cancers in China may stem from unsafe drinking water.

Recent studies have reported that emissions from China's export industries are worsening air pollution as far as the western United States. China's neighbors, including Japan and South Korea, have also expressed concern over acid rain and smog affecting their populations. Environmental ministers from the three northeast Asian countries agreed to boost cooperative efforts to curb air pollution and to protect water quality and the maritime environment in 2014.

The damage has also affected China's economic prospects as it continues to pursue extractive resources abroad, such as oil and other fossil fuels. Its economic partners, particularly in the developing world, face costly environmental burdens attached with doing business with China, write CFR Economy staff and Michael Levi in *By All Means Necessary*, their book on China's quest for resources.

Views of pollution and climate change in China

How big of a problem is ...

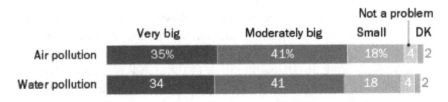

	Very big	Moderately big	Small	DK
Air pollution	35%	41%	18%	4 2
Water pollution	34	41	18	4 2

Is global climate change a very serious problem, somewhat serious, not too serious or not a problem?

	Very serious	Somewhat serious	Not too serious	DK
Climate change	18%	57%	19%	2 4

Note: Due to rounding, percentages may not total to 100%.
Source: Spring 2015 Global Attitudes survey.

PEW RESEARCH CENTER

Citizen Outrage

Environmental damage has cost China dearly, but the greatest collateral damage for the ruling Communist Party has likely been growing social unrest. Demonstrations have proliferated as citizens gain awareness of the health threats and means of organized protest (often using social media). In 2013, Chen Jiping, former leading member of the party's Committee of Political and Legislative Affairs said that environmental issues are a major reason for "mass incidents" in China—unofficial gatherings of one hundred or more that range from peaceful protest to rioting. Environmental protests in rural and urban areas alike—such as those in Guangdong, Shanghai, Ningbo, and Kunming—are increasing in frequency. The number of "abrupt environmental incidents", including protests, in 2013 rose to 712 cases, a 31 percent uptick from the previous year.

CFR's Economy points out that one of the most important changes in China's environmental protest movement has been a shift, beginning in the late 2000s, from predominantly rural-based protests to urban-based movements. The issue has worried the top leadership, which views the unrest as a threat to the party's legitimacy. "Air pollution in China has turned into a major social problem and its mitigation has become a crucial political challenge for the country's political leadership," write Center for Strategic and International Studies' Jane Nakano and Hong Yang. Yet the government has responded to public outcries: Chinese Premier Li Keqiang declared a "war on pollution" in March 2014; in May of the same year the government strengthened the country's Environmental Protection Law for the first time in twenty-five years. Such moves reflect "a changing understanding within China about the relationship between economic development and societal wellbeing," CFR Economy's staff and Levi write.

The Internet has played a crucial role in allowing citizens to spread information about the environment, placing additional political pressure on the government. In March 2015 *Under the Dome*, a TED Talk-style documentary on China's air pollution went viral, attracting hundreds of thousands of views before Internet censors blocked access, and in 2013 the discovery of thousands of dead pigs in the Huangpu river also spread rapidly online. However, experts say the jury is still out on the current government [implementing] meaningful reforms, which has shown more resolve in cracking down on public dissent than implementing environmental measures.

What's Being Done?

The government has mapped out ambitious environmental initiatives in recent five-year plans, although experts say follow-through has been flawed. In December 2013, China's National Development and Reform Commission, the top economic planning agency, issued its first nationwide blueprint for climate change, outlining an extensive list of objectives for 2020. Since January 2014, the central government has required fifteen thousand factories, including large state-owned enterprises, to publicly report real-time figures on air emissions and water discharges. The government also pledged to spend $275 billion over the next five years to clean up the air and $333 billion for water pollution. In a November 2014 joint statement on climate change with the United States, China committed to hit its peak carbon emissions by 2030 and to have renewables account for 20 percent of its energy mix by 2030. More recently, President Xi Jinping, on a state visit to Washington, announced that China would initiate a national cap-and-trade program in 2017.

> "What we're seeing now is an entirely new administration with an entirely different outlook on climate change."—Li Shuo, Greenpeace East Asia

China is one of the biggest investors in renewables, investing nearly $90 billion in 2014 as part of its pledge to cut its carbon intensity (far outspending the United States' $51.8 billion). Some analysts have predicted that China is on track to overtake the United States as the world's leading producer of wind energy by 2016. Meanwhile, Chinese firms continue to invest in and partner with international companies to develop renewable energy technologies.

Though policy implementation has been inconsistent, the environmental NGO community has grown to push the government to stay on track. Thousands of these groups—often working with U.S. and foreign counterparts—push for transparency, investigate corruption, and head grassroots campaigns. Friends of Nature is one of its oldest; Global Village and Green Home are among other well-known NGOs. Despite state support, these organizations inevitably face constraints from government fear that their activities could catalyze democratic social change.

Despite the political reforms needed to catalyze any real change in the environmental sphere, the response to China's crisis has triggered some optimism about the future. "What we're seeing now is an entirely new administration with an entirely different outlook on climate change," writes Greenpeace East Asia's Li Shuo. China, once reluctant to take a stand on environmental issues and climate change, emerged as a leader in negotiations at the 2015 UN Climate Conference in Paris where 195 countries signed a breakthrough accord. While China deserves due credit for its ambitious efforts to curtail its own environmental crisis, CFR Economy says it cannot be assumed that Beijing will follow through on its promises. "The proof will be on the ground—and of course, in the atmosphere."

China's Forest Conservation Program Shows Proof of Success

By Eva Botkin-Kowacki

The Christian Science Monitor, March 19, 2016

China appears to have turned the corner on deforestation. Beijing implemented a forest conservation program in 1998. And we now have proof that it's working. Logging and clear cutting shrank China's forests for decades, but from 2000 to 2010, the nation saw a net gain in tree cover, according to new data.

A team of scientists studied the nation's forests using satellite images, eyeing where tree cover expanded and decreased. Over the decade they saw significant recovery in about 1.6 percent of China's territory, while 0.38 percent continued to lose tree cover. Their findings are reported in a paper published Friday in the journal *Science Advances*.

"Before there was widespread deforestation," study author Andrés Viña of Michigan State University's Center for Systems Integration and Sustainability tells *The Christian Science Monitor* in an interview. "Now that has stopped and there is a net gain in forest cover." Forests harbor immense biodiversity, prevent soil erosion, and act as carbon sinks—scrubbing the atmosphere of carbon dioxide.

Trees grow by taking carbon dioxide from the atmosphere and locking it away in their roots, trunks, limbs and leaves until they die and decompose, when the carbon is released back into the atmosphere. Currently, elevated carbon dioxide levels in the atmosphere are heating up the planet. Forests are key, natural tools in mitigating climate change.

But forests have lost some 319 million acres, an area just larger than South Africa, over the past quarter century. Conservation programs like the one in China are starting to turn those trends around.

China's Conservation Program

For decades, Chinese forests were ravaged by the timber industry and clear cutting to convert areas to farmland. Biodiversity was lost, and flooding and soil erosion became significant issues without these trees to maintain the balance in the ecosystem. There was catastrophic fallout. Losses from flash flooding in the summer of 1998 alone reached $20 billion. In response, Beijing instituted the Natural Forest Conservation Program (NFCP).

The NFCP targeted sensitive regions that had been significantly degraded over the previous five decades, such as regions around the headwaters and other upstream portions of major rivers. A significant part of the NFCP has been extensive bans on logging in natural forests, instead shifting towards other timber sources.

From 1998 to 2000, the government had already invested over $2 billion in the conservation program. By the turn of the century, timber harvests from China's natural forests had been reduced from 32 million cubic meters (42 million cubic yards) in 1997 to 23 million cubic meters (30 million cubic yards) in 1999.

But that didn't mean China's thriving manufacturing industry was just going without timber. The nation now sees significant timber imports from places like Vietnam, Madagascar, and Russia, Dr. Viña says. "We think that success in reducing deforestation in China is basically being transferred into deforestation in other regions," he says.

"Over the long-term, sustainable forest management in China is important for forests in the rest of the world," says Robert Tansey, senior advisor for external affairs and policy in Northeast Asia and Greater China at The Nature Conservancy, who was not part of the study.

A Global Issue

"When it comes down to climate and carbon sequestration, these are global problems," Kevin Griffin, an ecologist at Columbia University's Lamont-Doherty Earth Observatory who was not part of this study, tells the *Monitor* in a phone interview. But this study just looked at China's success in forest conservation. Dr. Griffin says, "When you analyze them on national levels, you have to be mindful of the fact that savings in one country might mean a loss in another one." Viña agrees, "In this globalized world we need to go beyond national analysis. Now we have to go into international, cross-boundary analysis." Worldwide, the picture is less optimistic. Forest cover in many regions is still shrinking.

> **Currently, elevated carbon dioxide levels in the atmosphere are heating up the planet. Forests are key, natural tools in mitigating climate change.**

Although global deforestation has yet to reverse course, reports do suggest it is slowing. In fact, global deforestation rates have been cut in half since 1990, according to the United Nations Food and Agriculture Organization's Global Forest Resources Assessment (FRA). In the 1990s, an average of 0.18 percent of the world's forests were lost each year, but from 2010 to 2015, that average loss dropped to 0.08 percent.

"It is encouraging to see that net deforestation is decreasing and that some countries in all regions are showing impressive progress. Among others, they include Brazil, Chile, China, Cape Verde, Costa Rica, Philippines, Republic of Korea, Turkey, Uruguay, and Viet Nam," FAO Director-General Jose Graziano da Silva said in a press release in 2015. And with decreasing deforestation, that means more carbon storage. The FAO also reported that carbon emissions from forests decreased by 25 percent from 2001 to 2015.

Big Picture Or Whole Picture?

Narrowing in on one nation isn't the only limitation to this new study of China's forests, Griffin says. Satellite images can examine overall tree cover, but the picture is a lot more complex than simply counting trees and net forest mass. Different tree species and different types of forests can sequester more or less carbon or provide habitats for a different set of plants and animals, he says. And they might not be just the same as the degraded forests they're replacing.

For example, a recent study, published in the journal *Science*, shows that an expansion of forests towards dark green conifers in Europe has increased, rather than mitigated global warming. The findings challenge the widespread view that planting more trees helps human efforts to slow the Earth's rising temperatures. Apparently, not all trees have the same mitigating effect, reported the *Monitor*.

Although satellite imagery is "a really great tool to apply to a global problem" and the net increase in forest cover is a step in the right direction, the issue of regrowth is more complex than just simple snapshots, Griffin says. But generally, "knowing the status of our forests is super important," he says. "The forest provides an immense number of ecosystem services, everything from clean water and oxygen to habitat and biodiversity."

Mr. Tansey says, "Nature serves people's needs."

China Wants Cleaner Air—Without an Environmental Movement

By Simon Denyer

The Washington Post, **March 15, 2015**

Even by China's standards, it has been a contradictory couple of weeks on the environment.

First, a powerful documentary on air pollution, produced with official support, was released online and swiftly went viral, garnering more than 200 million views within days before being blocked by government censors. Today all references to the film have been scrubbed from the Chinese Internet, more effectively than the air ever could be.

On the sidelines of the annual meeting of the country's parliament, the National People's Congress, President Xi Jinping vowed to punish "violators" who destroy the environment "with an iron hand." Premier Li Keqiang opened the two-week-long NPC gathering by calling pollution "a blight on people's quality of life" and promised significant cuts in emissions.

On Sunday, he ended the meetings with a promise not to end his government's "war on pollution" until it reached its goal, and a pledge that the law would work "as a powerful, effective tool to control pollution—and would not be as soft as a cotton swab."

Yet as factories, trucks and oil companies continued to flout environmental regulations, police had different targets in their sights. On March 6, an activist in the southern city of Guangzhou who reposted information on social media about a planned gathering of "mothers concerned about the harm of smog" was arrested and put in detention for 14 days; two others were held overnight in Xi'an for brandishing placards blaming the government for the smog.

So is the government serious, or is it all a show? And if it really wants to improve the environment, what is wrong with a little public support and pressure?

The answers lie within the complex, many-headed nature of China's communist government and the huge challenges involved in addressing air pollution. The Communist Party, while obsessed with control and distrustful of public participation, recognizes that this is a huge touchstone issue for the urban middle class.

China is experiencing what Wang Tao of the Carnegie-Tsinghua Center for Global Policy in Beijing calls "the early tides of a sea change" when it comes to energy and the environment. Yet contradictions and power struggles are often at their sharpest when the tides are turning.

"The environment ministry certainly wants to get more power, and it can see huge pressure from the public for a better environment," he said. "But there is resistance from vested interests, and a power struggle over who should lead this process, in terms of policies and setting standards."

China burns more coal than the rest of the world combined, but last year—against expectations—coal consumption fell by 2.9 percent, its first decline in living memory.

Electricity generation by coal-fired power plants also fell for the first time in decades; coal- and steel-producing provinces that long sat at the top of the country's economic growth tables tumbled to the bottom of the pile.

Part of the reason is China's economic slowdown, which has hit heavy industry and the real estate sector hardest, and highlighted significant overcapacity. But government measures to cap coal and steel production, enforce stricter emissions targets and close down some illegal mines and furnaces have had an impact, too.

Enter Chai Jing, a well-known former anchor for state-run China Central Television, whose 104-minute long documentary *Under the Dome* was released online just days before the NPC meeting convened.

It was passionate and hard-hitting, well-researched and slickly produced.

Chai framed her concerns as the mother of a newborn girl, worried about the poisons her daughter and countless Chinese children were breathing in. Made with the support of officials from the Ministry of Environmental Protection, it exposed their powerlessness to set adequate standards and enforce those that exist. It described a ministry that was toothless against a steel industry that ignores environmental rules yet can't be challenged because it employs tens of millions of people; helpless against powerful state-run

> **The film also offered hope, in the experience of London and Los Angeles in cleaning the air without damaging the economy, and hope in the power of public participation to shame polluters.**

oil companies selling dirty fuel to raise their profits; and unable even to stop trucks belching thick plumes of smoke from infesting Beijing's streets.

But the film also offered hope, in the experience of London and Los Angeles in cleaning the air without damaging the economy, and hope in the power of public participation to shame polluters.

It was released February 28 and promoted by the state-run People's Daily Online Web site. By the next day, it had garnered 100 million views, even as the first instructions were being issued to state media outlets not to promote it.

The new environmental protection minister, Chen Jining, who had been parachuted into government from academia just a month before, sent Chai a text message that day congratulating her. He told reporters that the film reminded him of

Silent Spring, the 1962 book by Rachel Carson that inspired the U.S. environmental movement.

The film may not go down in history in quite the same way as Carson's book, not least because no comparable environmental movement will be allowed in China. Nor was it the first time that eyes had been opened here.

Still, Chai's film has informed and energized the debate, asking "questions that were on everybody's mind but had been suppressed," said Xiao Qiang, an adjunct professor at the University of California at Berkeley and founder of the *China Digital Times* Web site.

Yet by exposing some of the vested interests behind the smog, the film probably put important noses out of joint; its viral reception also may have shocked and frightened the party hierarchy.

While the initial social media reaction had been very positive, online attacks on Chai, both personal and factual, mounted in subsequent days. By March 6, censors ordered it removed from the Chinese Internet entirely: it can still be viewed on YouTube, with English subtitles, but that Web site is blocked in China.

Xi agreed to a landmark deal with President Obama last November to limit greenhouse gas emissions. The question now is how fast and how far he is prepared to move to address the issues raised by *Under the Dome*.

Xiao says the president's agenda is driven by a desire for popular support. But while addressing air pollution will win him credit among the middle class, Xi will be wary of undermining the economy and causing discontent in the country's industrial heartland, experts said.

Xi also will be wary of the risk that public unhappiness over the environment could translate into discontent with one-party rule. Yet environmentalists worry that a top-down approach to fighting pollution will be much less effective than one in which the public is allowed to participate.

"Xi needs popular support, but he is afraid of the public having real participation," said Xiao, adding, "The party won't let anything generate the public conversation or set the agenda without them driving it."

Why China and the US Have Found Common Purpose on Climate Change

By Jackson Ewing

The Conversation, **December 10, 2015**

Over the past year, the United States and China forged a climate change partnership that would have been almost unthinkable not long ago. Not only have both countries committed to emissions reduction and sustainable energy goals of substantial ambition, they are pursuing those goals in concert. This bilateral climate cooperation has been crucial to the UN climate summit in Paris and will continue to be so after any agreements are signed. Following years at loggerheads, the converging positions of the world's two largest emitters are becoming invaluable components of future climate response actions.

So why is this happening?

A combination of domestic, bilateral and international forces help explain the transformation, and reveal its potential and continuing challenges.

China's Pollution Crisis

In China, conventional pollution has moved environmental issues up the list of development priorities and made them part of the country's core national strategic calculations.

The scale and scope of protests against air pollution and environmental decline—which by some measurements lead to 1.6 million deaths per year—are on the rise, and Chinese leadership is responding through rhetoric and practice.

President Xi called poor air quality Beijing's "most prominent" challenge in 2014, while a top climate advisor deemed an acute pollution episode in the capital "unbearable."

In response, the metrics for measuring local bureaucratic success and promotions through party ranks emphasize environmental performance more than ever before. Punitive measures against polluters are gaining strength, and efforts to transform energy systems are accelerating through rapid expansions in solar, wind and nuclear sectors.

Such measures have the corollary effect of reducing greenhouse gas emissions, which has changed the ways that Chinese leadership views international pressure to act on climate change.

Outside pressures to reduce China's carbon emissions used to be viewed as anathema to the country's development needs, and a distraction from its core business of wealth genera-tion and societal develop-ment. They are now seen as opportunities for gain-ing partnerships, techni-cal support and finance to help China transition toward a cleaner energy future. This includes ex-panding China's manu-facturing and export of clean-energy technologies, which have strong economic growth potential.

> **Outside pressures to reduce China's carbon emissions used to be viewed as anathema to the country's development needs. . . .They are now seen as opportunities for gaining partnerships, technical support and finance to help China transition toward a cleaner energy future.**

Xi's China thus looks to the international climate arena for help addressing its domestic energy transition and pollution reduction goals. That the measures taken will also reduce climate risks is an added bonus.

US Executive Action

In the US, executive branch boldness has the Obama administration toeing the line of what is politically and legally tenable to advance some form of the environmen-tally progressive agenda the president campaigned on in 2008.

Frustrated with congressional intransigence and international inertia, the ad-ministration has opted for executive regulation at home and bilateral partnerships abroad. Obama's Clean Power Plan places new emissions standards on power plants and vehicles, mandates and supports clean energy expansion, and seeks to cut en-ergy waste and improve infrastructure.

On the first day of the Paris summit, the US announced Mission Innovation and officials touted the potential for technologies to lower emissions and "further encourage private-sector investment in clean energy innovation." And in defending its Clean Power Plan, the White House emphasizes public health dividends, job creation, economic growth and long-term energy security.

Like China, US leadership sees these measures as being in the country's long-term economic and strategic interests, and not merely as a ticket out of climate pariah status. Federal actions suggest this is not bluster, but a key part of the Obama administration's vision for the country's future.

Some Welcome Common Ground

Bilaterally, American and Chinese diplomats have come to see climate change cooperation as low-hanging fruit in an agenda otherwise brimming with strategic tension. From currency markets and competitive free trade groupings to mari-time navigation and the rise of China's military, the relationship does not lack for wicked problems.

Climate change used to be just another avenue for strategic posturing, with China clinging to its status as a developing country with little culpability for the problem, and the US justifying its inflexibility through China's inaction. Those days have passed, at least for now.

Beijing and Washington now see opportunity in the climate problem, and view it as a refreshingly non-zero sum game. They recently formed and now cofund the US-China Clean Energy Research Center, with a mandate extending through 2020, and are pursuing technical cooperation on issues from carbon capture and sequestration to sustainable urban infrastructure.

These connections feed into growing business ties, manifested most publicly through the annual US-China Clean Energy Forum. Such ties create incentives that are likely to keep climate cooperation from being a flash in the pan.

Global Enablers and Implications

This growing US-China alignment has accelerated because of changes in the direction of international climate change diplomacy.

UN-centric approaches have largely abandoned the holy grail of an encompassing and "binding" global agreement that covers an exhaustive range of climate issues. Disaggregated and largely voluntary approaches now rule the day, which allows the US and China to chart their own paths without feeling overly constrained or dictated to by international accords.

This shift also presents challenges. The US, China and their partners in Paris are searching for acceptable ways to transparently report and verify what emissions reductions are taking place where. This issue is taking on renewed urgency in the wake of China's revelations that it underreported past coal consumption, and that it may resist including strong verification protocols in the Paris agreement.

The US insists upon enhanced international norms and practices around verification, which it sees as essential to prevent the approach of voluntary commitments from becoming a house of cards. The two countries' ability to extend their cooperation to this issue will help determine the Paris outcome.

The US and China can likewise drive efforts to lubricate the gears of global commerce and reduce barriers to cooperation in clean energy sectors. Complex intellectual property and trade regulation challenges currently keep clean energy trade from reaching its full potential. These hurdles will not disappear overnight, but Paris is an appropriate forum for developing strategies to address them.

More fundamentally, the US and China are in a position to ensure that moves toward the flexible and voluntary do not devolve into reduced ambition and the shirking of loose commitments.

If these two economic and polluting behemoths show earnestness and ambition in Paris and beyond, the world is likely to follow.

Can the Chinese Government Get Its People to Like G.M.O.s?

By Christina Larson
The New Yorker, **August 31, 2015**

Food security is a national obsession in China. But the public remains wary of genetically modified crops.

In China, which has one-fifth of the world's population but just seven per cent of the world's arable land, food security is a national obsession. Pesticides and enhanced fertilizers no longer improve crop yields as markedly as they once did, and staple crops, such as rice, may not grow as reliably in the temperature extremes brought on by climate change. As a result, the government has begun to invest heavily in research on genetically modified crops. Last fall, the Communist Party's Literature Research Office published the text of a speech that President Xi Jinping had given before the Central Rural Work Conference, an agricultural-policy body, calling on domestic scientists to "boldly research and innovate, [and] dominate the high points of G.M.O. techniques." The most recent Five Year Plan names biotechnology, including enhanced agriculture, as one of seven "Strategic Emerging Industries."

Recently, I met with Caixia Gao, a prominent plant geneticist at the Institute of Genetics and Developmental Biology, in Beijing. For years, the institute's facilities were housed in a drab, Soviet-style building, but this spring they were expanded and renovated to include Ping-Pong tables, coffee lounges, and, on one floor, a so-called open lab with new microscopes, centrifuges, and other equipment that is shared among lab groups. (One young researcher, hunched over a petri dish, wrinkled her nose and wondered aloud whether the openness would foster collaboration or simply be distracting.) Gao ushered me into the new greenhouse, and her glasses quickly misted over from the sudden humidity. In 2009, after working in Denmark for a decade, Gao returned to China to lead a gene-editing research group under the Chinese Academy of Sciences. She has researched engineering rice for herbicide resistance and corn for drought resistance. Her recent work has involved editing out segments of the wheat genome in order to make the plant less susceptible to powdery mildew, a common fungal disease. (The condition can be controlled with fungicides, but these expose farmers to noxious chemicals.) Last year, her team's results were published in the journal *Nature Biotechnology*, where they attracted international attention. Gao pointed out a series of red clay pots, each containing spindly green wheat shoots, with strips of white tape around their brims. "The ones with labels have been genetically modified," she said proudly.

But, like many plant geneticists in China, Gao has yet to see her experiments on wheat, rice, or corn move beyond the lab or the greenhouse. For all of the government's investment, genetically modified food faces zealous public opposition and is largely banned from the marketplace. "The technology is getting better and more predictable, but the controversy is also getting bigger," Gao said. In 1997, China granted the first commercial license for a G.M. crop, cotton, which is now widely planted. The last commercial license, issued in 2006, went to papaya. Since then, commercial prospects have stalled; very few Chinese scientists have even received biosafety certificates to test the impact of G.M.O.s on the surrounding environment, a necessary step to evaluate safety before considering commercialization.

Zhang Qifa, one of the few scientists who did receive such experimental permission—in 2009, for Bt rice, which expresses a gene from the bacterium *Bacillus thuringiensis* that repels insect pests—has endured public attacks and threats to his personal safety. In 2010, as Zhang was delivering a lecture on G.M.O.s at China Agricultural University, in Beijing, a man in the audience threw a ceramic mug at him, narrowly missing. A woman in the audience yelled: "Zhang Qifa is a traitor!" Public anxiety about G.M.O.s has been stoked by people and organizations from across the ideological spectrum—by Greenpeace; by a Maoist group called *Wu You Zhi Xiang* (Utopia); by popular TV anchors speculating about horrible illnesses; and by expressions of general anti-Western sentiment. An online survey by the *China Daily* revealed that eighty-four per cent of respondents believe that genetically modified foods are unsafe.

The mixed messages over G.M.O.s reveal profound divisions within China's government, as well as an uncharacteristic sensitivity to public opinion. Much of the research has been funded through the Ministry of Science and Technology, with a mandate to elevate China's scientific prowess to world-class status. But the licenses for testing and final commercial approval are granted by a joint-ministerial conference made up of representatives from twelve agencies; it is convened by the Ministry of Agriculture, which is subject to State Council influ-

The chasm of credibility and the lack of a trusted referee make it hard for the public to sift rumor from fact.

ence and the imperative of maintaining "social stability"—that is, avoiding public unrest. "Put simply, the problem mostly lies in the rising resistance of the public to G.M.O.s, which has made the political leadership hesitant to go ahead with commercialization," Cong Cao, an expert in China's science policy at the University of Nottingham, in the United Kingdom, told me. President Xi's speech noted the schism: "We must be bold in studying [genetic modification, yet] be cautious in promoting it."

China is hardly alone in its popular worries. Recently, in the United States, when Chipotle moved to ban genetically modified ingredients from its burritos, the company initially attracted plenty of public praise. But a sharp backlash followed, drawing on the findings of mainstream research organizations, such as the American Medical Association, which have pointed out that there is no data to prove that eating G.M.O.s is bad for one's health. In China, science bloggers and state media outlets have often made the same point. But, because independent arbiters aren't allowed to thrive, the public doesn't believe them.

To live in modern China is to worry constantly about food safety. Scandals—from libidinous, corrupt officials to rigged TV talent shows—abound in the news and on social media, but few grip the public imagination like stories of poisoned food: the milk powder, tainted with the industrial chemical melamine, that killed at least six infants and sent more than fifty thousand ill babies to the emergency room in 2008; the watermelons that, in 2011, after receiving too much growth hormone, exploded; the admission, in 2013, by Guangdong's provincial government, that forty-four per cent of the local rice that had been tested was laced with dangerous levels of the heavy metal cadmium. The skeptical public has little faith that authorities will enforce food-safety regulations.

This mistrust makes it difficult to introduce new food technologies, even if China needs them. "If the government says that G.M.O. food is safe, Chinese people won't readily believe it," Sam Geall, an anthropologist at the University of Sussex who has been conducting field research recently in Beijing, told me. For the past eighteen months, Geall has been studying public opinion regarding G.M.O.s in China. The chasm of credibility and the lack of a trusted referee make it hard for the public to sift rumor from fact, he said: "This may be the clearest example where public opinion in China has likely played a role in stalling or stopping an innovation pathway that the government backs, for better or worse."

In many areas of national planning—from rerouting and damming the Yangtze River to clearing fields for the construction of airports and railways—China's leaders don't give much thought to public opinion. But food is personal, tangible, and essential. In recent years, ordinary Chinese citizens have gone to great lengths to avoid foods that they believe are inadequately regulated by the government. The smuggling of milk powder is on the rise, such that British supermarkets frequented by Chinese tourists have imposed limits on how many boxes a single customer can purchase. Geall's early research indicates that China's most educated citizens are among those most opposed to G.M.O.s; they want choices, especially where their dinner is concerned. Not even a government as powerful as Beijing's can force-feed a wary public.

China, U.S. Relationship Key in Climate Agreement

By Julie Makinen and Chris Megerian
The Los Angeles Times, December 13, 2015

Even as smog levels in Beijing often turn the sky a smoky gray, one thing was clear at the global climate change talks in Paris: China, once a laggard, emerged as a key player in the battle to help avert the worst effects of global warming.

The shift, by the world's largest emitter of greenhouse gases, helped pave the way for the commitment by nearly 200 nations to reduce emissions. "You had a developing country and somebody who had been leading the efforts against us," said Secretary of State John F. Kerry, "that opened the door."

After the December 2009 Copenhagen climate talks descended into chaos, some of the sharpest finger-pointing had been directed at China.

Beijing didn't send Premier Wen Jiabao to the final discussions that time, leaving leaders including President Obama and German Chancellor Angela Merkel to negotiate with an official who frequently left the room to phone his superiors. The Chinese pushed to remove specific targets on emissions cuts—even those that would apply only to advanced industrialized countries and not itself.

"China wrecked the talks ... and insisted on an awful 'deal' so Western leaders would walk away carrying the blame," British environmental author Mark Lynas, who was with one of the national delegations, wrote in a fly-on-the-wall account.

What a difference six years makes: Obama and Chinese President Xi Jinping appeared side by side at the start of this year's Paris climate change talks. And on Saturday, as global leaders congratulated themselves on reaching an agreement, the U.S. was singling out China for praise for its constructive engagement.

Asked after the vote to cite the most important steps along the way that enabled the deal, Kerry immediately pointed to China's willingness to "build a working partnership" with Washington and jointly announce national emissions-reduction targets in advance.

What explains China's shift? It's not necessarily pangs of guilt nor a newfound sense of global munificence. Instead, after years of downplaying its environmental crisis, Chinese leaders appear to have recognized that cleaning up China's toxic skies and pushing the country toward renewable energy are crucial to maintaining the Communist Party's grip on power amid rising public discontent.

Now, instead of regarding any multilateral environmental pact as a hindrance to unbridled economic growth, China sees an opportunity to seize agreements such as the Paris deal to showcase itself as a progressive superpower and responsible international stakeholder—while doing things it needs to do at home anyway.

The Obama administration, said Kerry, recognized this coming convergence in 2013 and sought to capitalize on it "to change the paradigm of what happened in Copenhagen."

"We saw they had environmental challenges in China and had [a self-] interest, therefore, and we tried to tap into that."

The alignment between China's domestic agenda and its willingness to step up in Paris was brought into sharp relief last week as air pollution levels skyrocketed in Beijing. For the first time, city officials issued a "red alert," closing schools, shutting down work at construction sites and ordering millions of cars off the capital's roads.

> **China has become the world's biggest investor in renewable energy and plans to launch a nationwide carbon emissions trading market in 2017.**

Since Xi came to power about three years ago, Chinese leaders have shown increasing political will to impose extraordinary measures to clean the skies, even if it means curtailing economic activity. To be sure, the steps have been uneven and at times downright vain—China has been most willing to shutter factories and curb coal burning when it's hosting high-profile international gatherings in Beijing such as the 2014 Asia-Pacific Economic Cooperation summit, September's military parade, and international sporting events.

Although the immediate goal is to protect public health, not halt global warming, the strictures generally target the same carbon-generators that cause global warming. At the same time, Chinese authorities are pushing the development of solar, wind, hydropower and nuclear power—and to make China's alternative energy sector a global economic force.

China has become the world's biggest investor in renewable energy and plans to launch a nationwide carbon emissions trading market in 2017.

These changes come as China increasingly acknowledges the human and financial toll of pollution. A 2014 joint study by the World Bank and China's government estimated that air pollution alone may cost the nation up to $300 billion a year. Another report led by economists and former foreign heads of state noted that smog is blamed for more than a million premature deaths annually in China, and said those deaths may cost the nation up to 13% of its GDP.

Sam Geall, a University of Sussex research fellow, said in a recent report that diplomacy certainly has helped push China along. "But far more important is the growing awareness that climate impacts and air pollution pose major threats to [China's] development," he said.

"In short, China's new approach rests on the fact that its leaders see combating climate change as being in the national interest," he added. "And underpinning that perception is not only a vision of how China might position itself in [the] future, but also a real transformation already underway in China's economy."

On the U.S. side, Obama has also become progressively bold, even as Congress shows resistance, said Eric Pooley, senior vice president for strategy and communications at the Environmental Defense Fund. With executive branch initiatives such as the EPA's Clean Power Plan—which takes effect this month and is designed to cut carbon emissions from power plants—Obama has been looking to make his environmental policies a centerpiece of his legacy.

That momentum is a contrast from 2009, when the president's eco-agenda had just suffered a defeat as the Waxman-Markey cap-and-trade bill failed in Congress, weakening his hand on the world stage.

Six years ago, "both of the biggest nations in the world were not ready to deal," Pooley said. Now, "the dynamic between the U.S. and China has totally changed. . . . They used to blame each other for inaction. Now they're encouraging each other toward more ambitious action."

In some ways, Washington and Beijing have been driven to find common ground on global warming because they have failed to see eye to eye on so many other issues, including trade and cyberattacks, as well as human rights and the South China Sea.

"China and the United States need an area where they can cooperate," said Nathaniel Keohane, a former Obama White House staffer and now vice president for global climate at the Environmental Defense Fund. "Climate change is becoming that area."

Momentum soared in November 2014 when Obama attended the APEC summit in Beijing and announced with Xi that the countries would both pursue policies to cut carbon emissions.

Obama pledged the U.S. would emit at least 26% less carbon in 2025 than it did in 2005. Xi vowed his country would "peak" its carbon emissions by 2030, if not sooner, and said solar, wind and other clean energy technology would account for 20% of China's total power production by that year.

Their bilateral agreement "sent a powerful signal to the rest of the world," said Alden Meyer of the Union of Concerned Scientists, a veteran of climate negotiations. "If the world's two biggest emitters aren't serious about dealing with the problem, you can't deal with the problem." Seeing them work together, he added, "gave people a sense of hope."

When Xi visited Washington in September, the two leaders followed up with a 17-point joint statement looking ahead to the Paris talks.

During negotiations in France over the last two weeks, U.S. officials were in "very, very regular contact with the Chinese," said one administration source, speaking on condition of anonymity. Though the two countries have real differences, administration officials said they believed they had mutual candor with the Chinese.

On Friday, as the Paris negotiators raced to hammer out the final language of their text, Xi and Obama once again spoke by phone.

The pact adopted Saturday for the first time commits virtually every nation to reducing the greenhouse gas emissions that cause climate change, and setting progressively more stringent goals every five years. Though each country will determine its own goals, nations will be required to submit to outside monitoring of their progress, and developed nations pledged to help fund new, clean energy sources for developing countries.

"With our historic joint announcement with China last year, we showed it was possible to bridge the old divide between developed and developing nations that had stymied global progress for so long," Obama said Saturday. "That accomplishment . . . was the foundation for success in Paris."

Environment for Development

By Jiang Nanqing
China Today, September 23, 2015

Accompanying unprecedented economic growth, a booming population, industrialization, and urbanization over the last few decades, China faces mounting environmental pressure. Climate change, loss of biodiversity, desertification, and unsustainable use of land, as well as global issues like energy, food, and water scarcity, hinder the country from reaching its poverty alleviation and sustainable development target. Therefore, the environment is one of the key areas of cooperation between China and the UN.

The United Nations Environment Programme (UNEP), founded in 1972 with its headquarters in Nairobi, Kenya, is the leading global environmental agency within the UN. Prior to the first United Nations Environment Assembly (UNEA) held in 2014, the 58-member governing body was reformed to universal membership (to include the full 193 member states of the UN), reinforcing the status and role of the UNEP.

In September 2003, the UNEP opened a liaison country office in Beijing—one of a handful of its kind. This move highlighted China's important status in dealing with global environmental issues, and promoted further cooperation between the UNEP and China.

Close Cooperation

During the 18th National Congress of the Communist Party of China (CPC) in 2012, China vowed to give high priority to ecological progress and incorporating it into building a beautiful country. It hence set the goal of sustainable development in line with the global trend.

"China admits it needs to rethink the role of the environment and that of its environmental sustainability dimension in future economic development," said Achim Steiner, executive director of the UNEP and under-secretary-general of the UN. He interpreted the notion of ecological progress in two respects: First, shifting to a green economy model doesn't entail a totally different mode of development; second, the rising cost of pollution abatement is increasingly affecting economic development.

Since the Chinese government signaled the economic transformation, UNEP has propelled policymaking in such fields as the environment, climate change, and science and technology through strategic partnership with the central and local governments. It also provided technical assistance to incorporating environmental issues into national strategy, facilitating implementation of a group of projects on issues from climate change, pollution abatement, and management of chemical materials, to resource efficiency, biodiversity and ecosystem protection, green economy, and South-South Cooperation.

Currently, the UNEP closely collaborates with the Ministry of Environmental Protection, National Development and Reform Commission, Ministry of Science and Technology, Ministry of Industry and Information Technology, and influential departments in other fields like the People's Bank of China. It also conducts full-scale cooperation with the municipal governments of Beijing, Guiyang, and Tianjin, research organs like the Chinese Academy of Sciences and the National Natural Science Foundation of China, and of course, the private sector. The UNEP has co-founded or sponsored an array of projects like the UNEP-Tongji Institute of Environment for Sustainable Development in 2002, the UNEP International Ecosystem Management Partnership in 2011, and the Global Efficient Lighting Center in 2012. All have become UNEP resource centers in China.

As an implementing agency of the Global Environment Facility (GEF), the world's largest public funder of environmental projects, the UNEP plays a key role in supporting countries to develop and execute GEF projects. In China, such projects cover a wide range of issues from climate change, biodiversity, and land deterioration, to trans-boundary waters and chemicals management.

The Chinese government is attaching increasing importance to high-level think tanks and their suggestions. UNEP Executive Director Achim Steiner serves as vice chairperson of the China Council for International Cooperation on Environment and Development (CCICED). He has offered advice on China's 13th Five-year Plan and sustainable development strategy. Steiner believes that the environmental issue shouldn't be segregated from other issues in China, as it is a systemic and long-term issue concerning economic development. As vice chairperson of the CCICED, he said he would assist international environmental specialists, Chinese experts and the government in discussing and researching China's environmental and development issues. He hoped to help test current environment policies in China to see if they are on the right ecological development track.

China's Green Economy

UNEP launched the Green Economy Initiative in 2008, calling on governments to increase investment in green industries to develop an economy featuring resource efficiency and social inclusion, which are precisely the targets of the Chinese government. Since 2009, UNEP and the Chinese government have jointly carried out research on the concept, investment, and indicator system of the green economy, and also the accounting system of the environmental protection industry. These studies objectively analyze the environment industry's potential contribution to economic growth, and also help bring the industry into the national accounting system.

UNEP is involved in the Partnership for Action on Green Economy (PAGE) project, jointly launched by five UN organizations—UNEP, United Nations Development Program (UNDP), United Nations Industrial Development Organization (UNIDO), International Labor Organization (ILO), and United Nations Institute for Training and Research (UNITAR)—aiming to solve the problems of multiple facets of the green economy. Cooperation among UN organizations makes it possible to cover major elements of this issue, and provide a comprehensive set of services and tools for developing a green economic strategy for countries.

> **Though faced with many environmental challenges, China has developed various low-cost, high-efficiency technologies and products, and accumulated experience in climate change mitigation and pollution abatement that fits other developing countries.**

In China, PAGE has chosen Jiangsu as a pilot province. The research team held rounds of discussions with relevant departments about problems, challenges, and demands when developing a green economy, and also carried out field research in cities like Nanjing and Zhenjiang. In collaboration with the provincial government, it analyzed investment and supporting policies and drew up a blueprint for Jiangsu's green development.

Sustainable energy is a key part of the green economy. When UN Secretary-General Ban Ki-moon launched "Sustainable Energy for All" (SE4ALL) in 2009, a series of platforms were established for accelerating the initiative in many fields, like district energy, building, transportation, lighting, and appliances. UNEP is actively engaged in two of the 11 action areas identified by SE4ALL—efficient lighting and vehicle fuel efficiency, and district energy. It is also taking responsibility for propelling it through the mode of public-private-partnership (PPP).

In 2012, the UNEP and China's National Lighting Test Center co-established the Global Efficient Lighting Center (GELC). The center's aim is to promote LED lighting and help set up related policies, standards, and quality inspection systems in African, Asian, and Pacific countries based on China's experience and technologies. In November 2014, the Global Efficient Lighting Forum was held successfully in Beijing. UNEP also positively conferred with the Chinese government and industrial partners to realize a leapfrog in the high-efficient home appliances and equipment market, which covers a range of electrical appliances and also electric vehicles and IT products. The aim is to reduce electricity consumption and slow the rate of climate change.

As China is stimulating domestic demands, sustainable consumption and production naturally becomes one of the key cooperation areas with the UNEP. As the secretariat of the 10-Year Framework of Programs on Sustainable Consumption and Production Patterns (10YFP), the UNEP advocated the CCICED's setting up of a research project on green consumption, and collaborated widely with Chinese cities, NGOs, and guilds to promote the concept. It has co-hosted China Sustainable Consumption Week annually since 2013.

South-South Cooperation

With fast economic growth, China is increasingly capable of helping other developing countries realize sustainable development through South-South Cooperation (SSC). "China and the World" has become a hot topic among offices of the UN system in China. SSC is one of the three key projects under the United Nations Development Assistance Framework in China. It also echoes the Belt and Road Initiatives recently put forward by the Chinese government.

Though faced with many environmental challenges, China has developed various low-cost, high-efficiency technologies and products, and accumulated experience in climate change mitigation and pollution abatement that fits other developing countries. It is expected that more Chinese cities, becoming aware of the environment's influence, will devote funds and expertise to the international promotion of sustainable economic development. These are opportunities for SSC.

Emerging countries like China are taking a leading role in SSC, said Achim Steiner. The senior environmental expert pointed out that less developed countries are no longer looking to developed countries for direction; instead, they would like to cooperate with each other, so becoming a new model of SSC. From this perspective, Steiner said, China's adoption of the path of green economy will profoundly influence the green economic transition across the world.

In 2012, the Chinese government contributed US $6 million to the UNEP's Trust Fund to support developing countries in building their capacity for environment management. On this basis UNEP offers support on an international level, including finding the most suitable technologies for countries, establishing technology transfer schemes and partnerships, and recognizing challenges.

The International Partnership on City Waste Water Technology Transfer is the best example. This project inspected over 40 kinds of sewage processing operations in more than 20 Chinese cities over a year. It meanwhile analyzed the demands of African and other less developed countries, and eventually set up last April the Asian regional hub for Global Wastewater Initiative in Beijing. The platform helps the docking between resources and demand by giving full play to information and technology sharing, so promoting SSC in wastewater processing.

In 2014, UNEP published UNEP Country Cooperation Framework on China (2014–2017), encompassing five sections including background, situation analysis, cooperation strategies, implementation means, and coordination and management. The following issues were listed in order of priority: propel the green economy in China, improve its environment capability and awareness, and assist and push forward the SSC. The framework will lay a solid foundation for further cooperation between China and UNEP.

China's Carbon Emissions May Have Peaked, but It's Hazy

By Edward Wong

The New York Times, April 3, 2016

A year and a half ago, negotiators from the United States persuaded the Chinese government to commit to a deadline for reversing the growth in greenhouse gas emissions from China.

The Obama administration portrayed the pledge as a major victory because China produces more of the gases that cause global warming than any other country, a quarter of the world's total. Though the deadline was far off, in 2030, environmentalists said the concession by Beijing was a significant breakthrough in efforts to coordinate a global response to climate change.

Now, some researchers examining recent energy data and the slowing Chinese economy are asking whether emissions of carbon dioxide, the main greenhouse gas, are already falling in China—more than a decade earlier than expected.

If so, there could be important consequences. China's success could energize worldwide efforts to limit global warming to 3.6 degrees Fahrenheit, or two degrees Celsius, above preindustrial levels, considered a difficult mission but critical for forestalling catastrophic environmental changes.

It could also put pressure on the United States and other nations to meet their own goals and set more ambitious ones. It would certainly blunt the argument made by those who say Washington should not make ambitious climate commitments because China is the world's main climate villain.

But determining if China's carbon emissions have peaked and are declining is difficult. Scientists measure emissions by extrapolating from official energy data and can provide only rough estimates for emissions from individual countries. Conclusions about whether a country's emissions have peaked are definitive only in hindsight, years after the fact. Even then, economic changes could result years later in a resurgence in emissions.

Problems with the accuracy of Chinese data make figuring out what is happening here particularly challenging. A paper published late last month by the journal *Nature Climate Change* warned that preliminary energy statistics from China were unreliable, and that "the most easily available data is often insufficient for estimating emissions."

Still, a handful of climate researchers say carbon emissions from China may be falling, after climbing rapidly since 2001, when China joined the World Trade Organization. Two British researchers, Fergus Green and Nicholas Stern, made this case in a paper published last month by the journal *Climate Policy*.

"It is quite possible that emissions will fall modestly from now on, implying that 2014 was the peak," they wrote.

Central to their argument are the possibility that China is undergoing an economic transformation and reports that coal use there has dropped or leveled off over the last two years. Industrial coal burning, by power plants and cement factories, for example, is the main source of carbon dioxide emissions in China.

> **"I would be more confident to say that China has reached a plateau or period of low growth," said Glen Peters, a scientist at the Center for International Climate and Environmental Research-Oslo. "I think to say 'peak' is a little bold."**

The decline in coal use is largely the result of China's economic slowdown. China's president, Xi Jinping, has said slower growth is the "new normal," and has been trying to shift the economy away from growth focused on heavy industry and toward growth fueled by consumer demand and the service sector, which is less carbon intensive.

China has also adopted policies to limit coal use around eastern population centers to battle air pollution, and has promoted alternative energy, including hydropower and nuclear power.

Together, these policies may be paying off faster than expected. Yang Fuqiang, a senior climate and energy adviser at the New York-based Natural Resources Defense Council, said carbon emissions from China may have peaked in 2014 at between 9.3 billion and 9.5 billion metric tons. (In the United States, emissions hit 6.1 billion metric tons in 2007 before falling, researchers for a Norwegian group said.)

A set of data revisions scheduled to be released this fall could show that emissions from China dropped by 1 to 1.5 percent last year, Mr. Yang said.

But there is also a strong case for less optimism.

Putting policy into effect has long been a problem in China, so it is unclear whether officials will follow through on Beijing's orders to move away from coal-burning industries. At the same time, China's leaders may balk at the painful steps needed to overhaul the economy. Restructuring efforts have already resulted in protests against mass layoffs.

Another question is energy use. Electricity demand in China is expected to continue growing, and the easiest way to meet it will be through coal-burning power plants rather than alternative energy sources.

China's coal-burning plants are operating below 50 percent capacity, and a recent Greenpeace East Asia report found that local officials issued permits for the construction of 210 more plants last year. Some of these projects could be suspended under new orders from Beijing, but activists are worried that China's electrical grid will continue to favor coal-based enterprises.

Oil and natural gas use is also rising in China—from people driving cars, for example—and the growth of carbon emissions from that could exceed the drop in emissions from coal use.

"I think the total of China's carbon dioxide emissions will rise again in coming years," said Jiang Kejun, a senior researcher at the Energy Research Institute of China's main economic planning agency.

Other skeptics note that Chinese cities are still growing. More than 55 percent of the population lives in cities now, but the government has set a goal of 60 percent by 2020. Urbanization means more construction and reliance on heavy industry, not to mention increased traffic.

"Most Chinese cities are building out," and more data on the impact is needed to figure out if carbon emissions have started falling for good, said Angel Hsu, an assistant professor at the Yale School of Forestry and Environmental Studies.

Chai Qimin, a senior director at China's National Center for Climate Change Strategy and International Cooperation, said the experience of other nations suggested that emissions would continue to rise because China's economy was still developing.

Most countries see carbon emissions fall when per capita gross domestic product climbs to between $20,000 to $40,000, but China's is still below $10,000, he said. "China has more industrialization and urbanization to do, which needs energy," he said.

Some researchers say China could be in a period in which emissions fluctuate for several years before a sustained decline, as they did in the United States before 2007.

"I would be more confident to say that China has reached a plateau or period of low growth," said Glen Peters, a scientist at the Center for International Climate and Environmental Research-Oslo. "I think to say 'peak' is a little bold."

Whether or not emissions from China are already falling, most researchers agree they will reach a peak no later than 2025, five years ahead of Beijing's pledge.

China also appears to be overshooting its goals for reducing carbon intensity, or the amount of carbon dioxide emitted per unit of economic output. China had set a goal of bringing carbon intensity down 40 percent to 45 percent below 2005 levels by 2020, mostly by shifting the economy away from heavy industry and fossil fuels.

But officials and researchers now say that a 50 percent cut by 2020 is possible, and that the government may revise its target to make it more ambitious.

"If China can revise this, then I'd be very happy," Mr. Yang of the Natural Resources Defense Council said. "China would be playing a leadership role in climate change."

3
Human Rights, Citizen Workers, and Dissidents

Chris McGrath/Getty Images News

A pro-democracy activist holds a yellow umbrella in front of a police line on a street in Mongkok district on November 25, 2014 in Hong Kong.

Personal Rights and Human Rights

Though the overall relationship between China and the United States has improved since the end of the Cold War, opinion polls indicate that most Americans have a relatively low opinion of China's government, believing that the government is guilty of numerous human rights abuses. Among other accusations, critics of China argue that the Chinese government monitors and censors the press, Internet, and academic research, and places strict limits on the population's freedom of expression, assembly, and religion. The Chinese government has also been accused of supporting discrimination against China ethnic and religious minorities and of using excessive force, torture, and violence in police/military operations. Similarly, Chinese opinion polls indicate that Chinese citizens are critical of the U.S. government's military operations and the nation's history of racial and class violence. Evidence of China's human rights violations has become more readily available in the digital age, leading to widespread public criticism within the international community. China has responded to international criticism by arguing that foreign powers highlight China's existing social/governmental challenges while ignoring the Chinese government's attempts to improve the lives of the Chinese people. In comparison to the United States, Chinese culture places reduced emphasis on individual freedoms and greater emphasis on an individual's function within society. This fundamental philosophical difference has exerted a major influence on Chinese governance throughout history.

The Accusations Against China

In 1949, with the official establishment of the People's Republic of China, the Chinese Communist Party established ten legal documents outlining "citizen's rights" for the population. However, the authoritarian regime that controlled China through the 1960s and 1970s, provided little real human rights protections. As the Chinese government began opening up to foreign visitation and trade in the 1970s, the Chinese population became more familiar with foreign human rights standards, initiating a human rights movement within China. There was a government backlash against foreign "pollution" in the mid- to late-1980s, but the international community began exerting greater pressure on the Chinese government to liberalize after the 1989 Tiananmen Square incident in which a pro-democracy student movement ended in a government crackdown resulting in the death of hundreds of protesters and a period of martial law.[1]

International human rights organizations and Chinese activist organizations accuse the Chinese government of targeting, harassing, and imprisoning activists who speak out against the government's repressive policies and human rights violations. For instance, in February of 2016, the activist organization Human Rights In

China (HRIC) reported on a governmental crackdown on defense lawyers working on cases seen as critical of governmental policy, allegedly resulting in the imprisonment, without due process, of hundreds of Chinese legal activists.[2] Numerous high profile cases, such as the 11-year imprisonment of human rights activist and Nobel Peace Prize winner Liu Xiaobo demonstrate the Chinese government's aggressive approach to curtailing political opposition.[3]

Activist group Human Rights Watch also alleges that Chinese police regularly torture suspects in detention. In a 2010 case, a Chinese man, Zhao Zuohai, claimed that torture while in police custody led him to confess to a murder he had not committed, spending 11 years in prison before evidence surfaced that overturned his conviction. Human Rights Watch alleges that such abuses occur frequently in China[4] while the Chinese government restricts media access to the nation's prison and police facilities, thus making reliable data difficult to obtain.

The Chinese government is also frequently accused of maintaining discriminatory policies against minority ethnic and religious groups. The Falun Gong spiritual movement, for instance, has been banned in China since 1999, with practitioners reportedly being frequently arrested and imprisoned for practicing the banned faith. Muslims have also been persecuted in China, especially in the Xinjian autonomous region where separationists representing the nation's Muslim Uighur population have engaged in violent clashes with police. The treatment of China's Uighur is problematic, as some separationist groups within the Muslim minority have alleged ties to radical Islamic organizations. Hundreds of Uighurs in Western China have reportedly been killed by the police and Chinese military since 2009.[5] China's ongoing occupation of Tibet is another international human rights concern and a number of activist organizations report that the Chinese government continues to execute activists and protestors demonstrating against the occupation or in favor of Tibetan independence.

In addition to military and police abuse, U.S. politicians and rights groups have criticized the government's approach to personal liberties, including freedom of expression, the press, and assembly. The Chinese government censors Internet and postal communication and restricts access to certain websites seen as dangerous or otherwise unfit for public consumption. In 2015, the Internet Rights group Freedom Net ranked China last of 65 nations in terms of Internet freedom, and accused the Chinese government of conducting unwarranted surveillance, removing content from websites, and of arresting and harassing individuals for attempting to share information deemed critical of Chinese governmental policies.[6] In addition to censorship, there have been numerous reports indicating that the Chinese government has imprisoned journalists and writers for publishing articles criticizing the government or the Communist party.

Labor rights are another major issue in China, as the Chinese government does not allow independent labor organizations. Human rights and labor rights organizations have accused the Chinese government of allowing companies to exploit laborers without providing safe working conditions or adequate pay, and have accused the government of using violence and intimidation to prevent the formation of labor reform protests. Despite the threat of arrest or violence, labor groups have emerged in China using social media to organize protests against unfair wages and unsafe working conditions. Though private labor unions are illegal, the emerging labor movement in China has strong ties to the ruling political party, thus making labor reform one of China's most controversial issues.[7]

Human Rights in the United States

In 2015, the U.S. State Department released its annual report on global human rights, containing indictments of China's record of detention, censorship, and police abuse. The Chinese government responded by criticizing the United States of supporting widespread racial violence and discrimination and of failing to prevent gun violence and the spread of illegal weapons.[8] Rights organizations like Amnesty International and Human Rights Watch agree, in general, with some aspects of the human rights allegations made by the Chinese government. Most recently, the Ferguson protests of 2015 highlighted the existence of persistent racial prejudice and bias within the U.S. police and judicial systems. Examinations of the U.S. justice system have found, for instance, that minority suspects are more likely to be stopped by police, arrested, tried, and convicted than white offenders suspected or arrested for similar crimes. Rights organizations also criticize the U.S. government for failing to address issues involving the condition of U.S. prisons and the government's treatment of immigrants, especially in regards to the detainment and deportation of unauthorized migrants.[9]

China is not the only foreign government to criticize U.S. government policy. Within the international community, for instance, the United States has been accused of using the threat of terrorism to bolster the nation's control over international trade and extend U.S. military influence. Some foreign politicians have also criticized U.S. military aggression due to the number of civilian casualties resulting from U.S. anti-terrorism operations. Though exact figures on the number of combatants and civilians who have been killed in the U.S.-led War on Terror are lacking, some media and medical organizations have estimated that between 2 and 4 million have died in the ongoing conflict.

In addition to criticisms of U.S. human rights and military policies, the United States has been criticized for exploiting labor laws and poverty in developing nations to further U.S. economic interests. For instance, in 2006, when the Chinese government was debating a law to discourage the formation of sweatshops and protect worker's rights by reducing restrictions on unionization, a number of U.S. corporations opposed the law and threatened to build fewer factories in China.[10] Therefore, while the U.S. government openly opposes China's labor and civil rights laws, U.S. corporations and the government continue to take advantage of favorable economic conditions, even as such activities further the exploitation of disadvantaged populations.

Perspectives and Opinions

A Pew Research Survey from March of 2016 indicated that Americans and Chinese have relatively low opinions of one another. The report found that only 38 percent of Americans view China favorably, while 44 percent of Chinese view the United States favorably. A majority in both nations believe that China will overtake the United States as the world's most powerful economic power, while 54 percent of Chinese citizens believe that the United States has attempted to prevent China's economic advancement. On the whole, American citizens are far more likely to be concerned about China's economic influence and the large amount of Chinese debt than by the nation's human rights record.[11] In China, citizens were most concerned about governmental corruption, air and water pollution, though human rights was a significant concern.[12]

In a 2013 article in *The Atlantic*, Nicholas Bequelin of Amnesty International's Hong Kong office argued that the United States must strive to provide the best possible human rights example for developing nations, including the powerful but still developing China. In terms of U.S.-China relations, Bequelin argued further that the United States should alter its relationship with China, making human rights improvements a requirement for future economic or trade agreements. Columbia University political science professor Andrew Nathan argued that urging China to improve its treatment of citizens can also encourage foreign business by making travelers feel more comfortable visiting and conducting business in China. The expansion of diplomatic contact between the United States and China in the 2010s may make it possible for the United States to influence Chinese human rights policies in the future. As Bequelin argues, however, U.S. influence may be stronger if the U.S. government also strives to address domestic concerns, thus helping to make the United States an example of responsible and advanced human rights policy.

Micah L. Issitt

Recommended Reading

"6 Facts About How Americans and Chinese See Each Other." *Pew Research*. Pew Research Project. Mar 30 2016. Web. 25 Apr 2016.

Barboza, David. "China Drafts Law to Boost Unions and End Abuse." *New York Times*. New York Times Company. Oct 13 2006. Web. 25 Apr 2016.

"China Issues Report Attacking US Human Rights Record." *The Guardian*. Guardian News and Media. Jun 26 2015. Web. 25 Apr 2016.

Chunying, Xin. "A Brief History of the Modern Human Rights Discourse in China." *Human Rights Dialogue*. Dec 4 1995. Web. 25 Apr 2016.

"Freedom on the Net 2015." *Freedom House*. Freedom House. 2015. Web. 25 Apr 2016.

"Mass Crackdown on Chinese Lawyers and Defenders." *Hrichina*. Human Rights in China. Feb 5 2016. Web. 25 Apr 2016.

Ruz, Camila. "Human Rights: What Is China Accused Of?" *BBC News*. Oct 21 2015. Web. 24 Apr 2016.

Tang, Didi. "China's 168 Million Migrants Workers Are Discovering Their Labor Rights." *Business Insider*. Apr 6 2015. Web. 25 Apr 2016.

"Tiger Chairs and Cell Bosses." *HRW*. Human Rights Watch. May 13 2015. Web. 25 Apr 2016.

"Why Is There Tension Between China and the Uighurs?" *BBC*. BBC World. Sep 26 2014. Web. 25 Apr 2016.

Wike, Richard and Bridget Parker. "Corruption, Pollution, Inequality Are Top Concerns in China." *Pew Global*. Pew Research Center. Sep 24 2015. Web. 25 Apr 2016.

"World Report 2015: United States." *HRW*. Human Rights Watch. 2015. Web. 25 Apr 2016.

Notes

1. Chunying, "A Brief History of the Modern Human Rights Discourse in China."
2. "Mass Crackdown on Chinese Lawyers and Defenders."
3. Ruz, "Human Rights: What Is China Accused Of?"
4. "Tiger Chairs and Cell Bosses."
5. "Why Is There Tension Between China and the Uighurs?" *BBC*.
6. "Freedom on the Net 2015," Freedom House.
7. Tang, "China's 168 Million Migrants Workers Are Discovering Their Labor Rights."
8. "China Issues Report Attacking US Human Rights Record."
9. "World Report 2015: United States," Human Rights Watch.
10. Barboza, "China Drafts Law to Boost Unions and End Abuse."
11. "6 Facts About How Americans and Chinese See Each Other," Pew Research.
12. Wike and Parker, "Corruption, Pollution, Inequality Are Top Concents in China."

China's Latest Crackdown on Workers Is Unprecedented

By Michelle Chen

The Nation, December 18, 2015

In an unprecedented crackdown on some of China's most effective independent labor organizations, known as worker centers, seven worker-activists have been detained and held virtually incommunicado in detention facilities in Foshan and Guangzhou.

The detainees include Panyu Dagongzu Service Center staffers Zeng Feiyang and Zhu Xiaomei; former Dagongzu staffers Tang Jian (aka Beiguo) and Meng Han; Peng Jiayong of the Panyu-based Laborer Mutual Aid Group; He Xiaobo, director of Foshan Nanfeiyan Social Work Services Organization; and Deng Xiaoming of the Haige Workers Center. Beiguo reportedly remains detained, but his whereabouts are unconfirmed as of December 16.

The activists are reportedly being detained on grounds of "endangering national security," according to Amnesty International. It is unclear whether charges have been formally brought; earlier reports indicated Zeng and Zhu had been apprehended on lesser charges of "disrupting social order," and He charged with "embezzlement." Attorneys, restricted from communicating with them, have demanded clarification on the charges. The national-security charges, Amnesty reports, "could lead to a sentence of up to 15 years imprisonment."

Advocates report that He and Zhu's lawyers, along with detainees' family members, have been arbitrarily barred from visiting. And Zhu, a former migrant worker from Henan turned organizer, has been denied bail and is unable to reunite with the baby she is nursing. Authorities have also reportedly questioned and harassed dozens of relatives and affiliates of the detainees and their groups.

While the government remains mum on the detentions, the police sweep seems an unusually harsh crackdown on community-based groups that have long struggled to balance mutual aid and advocacy without courting controversy. Working outside the international spotlight and concentrated in China's gritty southern manufacturing belt, organizers toil thanklessly each day on behalf of local workers: filing complaints, winning back wages, fostering collective bargaining, and occasionally mediating strikes and other workplace conflicts.

But this is not the first security clampdown these activists have experienced. The website China Change has detailed the activists' often tumultuous career as rank-and-file organizers. Zeng, a former corporate lawyer turned grassroots labor organizer, was detained and threatened by police, and later attacked by unidentified assailants, after helping to coordinate a major strike at a Guangdong shoe factory in late 2014.

Peng Jiayong, a veteran labor activist who became a full-time grassroots rabble-rouser after he was fired for trying to organize coworkers at a foreign-owned company, was assaulted by "eight unidentified men and severely injured" last April, according to China Change.

But what makes these activists so dangerous? Unlike the Ai Weiwei school of celebrity dissenters known worldwide for their subversive spectacles, Nee says, worker centers are comparatively low-key and pragmatic. They typically prefer to use arbitration and negotiation with management, rather than direct action like strikes, which they would generally treat "as a tactic of last resort."

> Still, though the targeted groups face challenges from the state and business, a global groundswell of solidarity has emerged to defend the detainees as symbols of a labor movement that is as vital as it is endangered.

Coinciding with wider crackdowns on journalists and activist lawyers, the detentions might signal an effort to tighten the government's stranglehold on civil society. One veteran labor activist, commenting anonymously on a Hong Kong commentary site, explained that "the raids were well planned from a higher level of government," and that facing an economic slump, by targeting activists who were "promoting a positive attitude to the workers' collective bargaining," the government was actively suppressing "the legitimate aspirations of workers."

Meanwhile, a wave of labor unrest is roaring across southern China. According to the watchdog group China Labour Bulletin, labor protest incidents in Guangdong have recently spiked, from 23 in July to 56 in November, mostly in manufacturing workplaces where workers protested over unpaid wages, "factory closures, mergers and relocations."

Elsewhere in Guangdong, Walmart store workers are escalating their long-running struggle to defy the government-run union apparatus, the All-China Federation of Trade Unions (ACFTU), by campaigning for independent candidates. While their actions are not directly connected to the NGO crackdown, their struggle for independent unionization underscores the challenges of building autonomous rank-and-file power in China's increasingly globalized and precarious workforce.

Both the silencing of worker centers and Walmart's insurgent union drive point to growing tensions between independent labor activism and the management-aligned official union system. In many workplace disputes, according to CLB's research brief on China's labor movement, labor unrest has outgrown the ACFTU bureaucracy, which typically serves to neutralize disputes on management's behalf. In recent years, workers "have been perfectly able and willing to bypass the trade union entirely and organize strikes and protests themselves in their pursuit of better pay and conditions."

"The union doesn't do anything" to promote workers' interests, according to Hong Kong–based labor scholar Anita Chan. A lack of strong unions, she adds, is one reason groups like Dagongzu have approached labor relations through "legalistic" rather than militant means.

Over the past decade of reform-era union activity, Chan says, grassroots organizing has been impeded by an oppressive political climate. Even in larger worker uprisings, such as last year's massive Yue Yuen shoe-factory strikes, protests have been co-opted by union officialdom or quashed by authorities, and haven't engendered sustainable autonomous organizing campaigns.

"All these strikes, they're directed against management, not against the state," she observes.

Still, though the targeted groups face challenges from the state and business, a global groundswell of solidarity has emerged to defend the detainees as symbols of a labor movement that is as vital as it is endangered.

In the Hong Kong Confederation of Trade Unions' online petition, signed by numerous human-rights groups and European and Asian labor organizations, the union's globalization monitor, "The Chinese government purports to advance the 'rule of law' within its borders and promotes the idea of a civilized and peaceful rise internationally. However, local governments abuse their power, using violence and arrests to repress and intimidate labour organizations, preventing Chinese workers from pursuing fundamental labour rights."

In Nee's view, the support for the detained activists stems from solidarity as well as from gratitude for the role of the worker centers in movement building and training rank-and-file organizers. "A lot of the reason why the strikes [and protests] have succeeded," he says, "is because of worker solidarity and a new rights consciousness. . . . Once people are aware of their rights, it's kind of hard to go back unless you permanently try to silence them."

The persecution of Guangdong's worker-activists exposes the hypocrisy of China's "rule of law." Nonetheless, it also reveals an emergent political landscape for labor: While the state can suppress individual activists, the consciousness of workers is rising too fast for anyone to contain it.

China Cracks Down on Rights Figures with Subversion Charges

By Josh Chin

The Wall Street Journal, **January 15, 2016**

Chinese authorities signaled a return to an earlier, more strident era of social control this week by formalizing the arrests of several long-detained human-rights lawyers and activists on suspicion of subversion.

The use of subversion, a political crime that carries a possible life sentence, marks a dramatic escalation in the Chinese government's campaign to choke off sources of potential dissent, activists say. It comes as slowing economic growth threatens to exacerbate social tensions in the world's most-populous country.

Police delivered formal arrest notices to the families of at least 11 lawyers, legal assistants and activists who had been in custody since being rounded up in a nationwide sweep in early July, according to human-rights groups. Well-known human-rights lawyers Wang Yu and Zhou Shifeng were among those arrested on suspicion of subversion. They couldn't be reached, but their supporters rejected the charges as trumped up.

Beijing also confirmed this week that it had detained a Swedish citizen, Peter Dahlin, on suspicion of endangering state security. Mr. Dahlin, the co-founder of a nonprofit called the China Urgent Action Working Group that works with Chinese human-rights lawyers, disappeared while on his way to the Beijing airport in early January, the nonprofit said in a statement, which described the charges as baseless.

China's Foreign Ministry said on Wednesday that the country would protect Mr. Dahlin's rights and facilitate Sweden's performance of its consular duties. On Thursday, Swedish embassy spokeswoman Gabriella Augustsson said the embassy had requested to visit a Swedish citizen detained in China but "so far this request has not been met."

This week's arrests and detentions suggest Chinese authorities have grown fed up with the challenge posed by the country's increasingly confrontational community of human-rights lawyers. Many [of] those arrested are members of a group of self-described "die hard" lawyers who employ unorthodox tactics, including pressing their clients' cases online and in the streets, in doing battle with often hostile courts.

"A political decision was made that lawyers doing their job in this way was something the authorities couldn't tolerate," said Eva Pils, an expert in Chinese law and human rights at King's College London. "It's incompatible with the goals of the state."

Chinese authorities have moved aggressively against government critics under Chinese President Xi Jinping. But until recently they have tended to charge targets of their crackdown with minor offenses like tax evasion or disturbing public order—an attempt, many activists say, to be seen as less draconian.

In threatening multiple people with serious political charges, the government appears to be dusting off the harsher approach used under Mr. Xi's predecessors, according to Lu Jun, a veteran antidiscrimination activist who has worked with many of those detained in the roundup.

"I'm shocked, to be honest. This is a major shift," Mr. Lu said, referring to the arrests this week. "In the past, even if someone was charged with subversion, it was for inciting subversion. Straight subversion without the 'inciting' part becomes very, very serious."

U.S. State Department deputy spokesman Mark Toner this week repeated American calls for the charges to be dropped and the detained lawyers and activists to be released. China's Foreign Ministry on Thursday rejected that, saying they were being investigated according to law. Chinese authorities haven't otherwise commented on the arrests.

Some supporters trace the crackdown on lawyers to the case of Wu Gan, a prominent activist employed by the Fengrui law firm. Mr. Wu, who goes by the nickname Super Vulgar Butcher online, was detained and then formally arrested last year on suspicion of inciting subversion after he discovered video footage that contradicted government accounts of a controversial police shooting in the country's northeast.

Wang Yu, who was among the lawyers who attempted to defend Mr. Wu, was detained on July 8 on her way to the Beijing airport a few days after he was formally arrested. Two days later, police rounded up hundreds of other lawyers and activists, eventually detaining two dozen, in an action that has come to be known in Chinese human-rights circles as "Black Friday."

"That case was the fuse," said Mr. Lu, the antidiscrimination activist, said of Mr. Wu's arrest. "Though the crackdown was probably only a matter of time."

Ms. Wang's lawyer said police had illegally denied his requests to visit his client and told him that she had chosen someone else to represent her. Police didn't say who her new lawyer was.

> **This week's arrests and detentions suggest Chinese authorities have grown fed up with the challenge posed by the country's increasingly confrontational community of human-rights lawyers.**

"From the beginning, this entire episode has been completely abnormal, completely illegal," said the lawyer, Wen Donghai. "They're doing everything they can to push lawyers out of the process."

Ms. Wang and most of the others detained in last year's sweep were being held in the coastal city of Tianjin, according to Chinese Human Rights Defenders, a

U.S.-based group that has been monitoring the crackdown. Tianjin police referred questions to the city prosecutor's office. Repeated calls to the prosecutor's office rang unanswered Thursday and Friday.

Once a fractured group, human-rights lawyers have also grown increasingly cohesive and willing to support each other in clashes with authorities, Ms. Pils said.

A pivotal event occurred in 2013, when one Fengrui lawyer ordered detained for 10 days by a court in eastern China's Jiangsu province for insisting he be allowed to photograph a document while defending of member of the banned Falun Gong religious group. News of the detention spread through social media to other lawyers, who mounted online and offline protests that ended with Mr. Wang's early release.

State media reports following the Black Friday sweep accused the lawyers of illegally disrupting legal processes on numerous occasions, including by staging protests outside courthouses and being overly confrontational in court. The state-run Xinhua News Agency reported in late July that Zhou Shifeng, a partner at Fengrui, had confessed the firm broke the law in defending some of its clients.

Some lawyers who were interrogated during the sweep but not detained said they believed the harsh treatment of their colleagues stemmed from concerns in Beijing over turbulence in the country's previously supercharged economy. China is widely expected to announce its slowest annual economic growth in more than two decades when it releases 2015 GDP figures next week. Layoffs and factory closings fueled a doubling of labor protests in the first 11 months of last year, according to Hong Kong-based civic group China Labor Bulletin.

"They're worried a slowdown in growth will engender all kinds of dissatisfaction, factories closing, people losing jobs. So they're cracking down on human-rights lawyers and human-rights leaders ahead of time," said one human-rights lawyer who was interrogated during the Black Friday roundup.

Tang Jitian, another human-rights lawyer, said that there wasn't enough evidence to convict any of the detained lawyers of subversion and that the point in arresting them was to create a climate of fear for other lawyers.

The effects of the crackdown could be felt beyond the relatively small circle of human-rights lawyers, Ms. Pils said.

"This is a much more serious attack, not just on human-rights lawyers, but on civil society more widely and the very idea of a legal system in which lawyers are expected to play a forceful advocacy role," she said.

Mr. Dahlin, the Swedish nonprofit worker, is the first foreigner to be formally detained on state security in connection with human-rights lawyers. Michael Caster, a colleague of Mr. Dahlin's, said the Swede's detention "makes a mockery of President Xi Jinping's stated commitments to the rule of law."

Why Did China Kidnap Its Provocateurs?

By Barbara Demick
The New Yorker, February 16, 2016

Last October 17th, Gui Minhai, the publisher of Mighty Current Media, in Hong Kong, returned from grocery shopping to his seaside condominium in Thailand and found a young man waiting for him at the front gate. Gui chatted with the man for a few minutes, and then drove off with the young man in his own white hatchback, but not before asking the doorman to leave the groceries in the hall outside his apartment. The implication was that he would be back shortly. He never came back.

Two months later, Lee Bo, who with Gui Minhai was a co-owner of Mighty Current and ran the company's Hong Kong bookstore, stayed late at work, preparing a large book order he was supposed to deliver to a client. Closed-circuit footage from the office elevator showed him speaking to a young man in a cap. When he didn't come home for dinner as expected, his wife called the police.

On January 11th, Li Xin, a Chinese dissident journalist, was on a train in northern Thailand heading toward the border with Laos. He was staying in Thailand while seeking political asylum, and needed to leave the country to renew his tourist visa. "Left the train and heading toward the border," he texted his wife. Then he vanished.

The mysteries, which Jiayang Fan wrote about in early January, have since been solved. All three men were kidnapped to China for political offenses: publishing information embarrassing to the Communist Party. Each man later made calls or sent messages to family claiming he had returned to China "voluntarily"; these claims are widely believed to have been made under duress. Three other men involved with Mighty Current Media vanished shortly after Gui Minhai, although it appears that they were seized while on the mainland.

China's treatment of its critics is notorious. Between July and September of last year, two hundred and eighty human-rights lawyers and activists were detained, according to Human Rights Watch. The extralegal methods used in these recent cases go even further: they are tantamount to kidnappings. Thailand, of course, is a sovereign country. Hong Kong has its own legal system, enshrined by the treaty that allowed its 1997 handover from Britain. Because of distrust of China's legal system, Hong Kong does not have a rendition agreement with the mainland.

The Chinese are not the first to resort to extraordinary rendition. The most famous case was the Israeli abduction of Adolf Eichmann from Buenos Aires, in 1960, to stand trial for war crimes. After the September 11, 2001, attacks, the Central Intelligence Agency picked up at least a hundred and thirty-six terrorism suspects and moved them to secret locations around the world for interrogation and often torture.

The men recently abducted by China were not suspected war criminals or terrorists. With one possible exception, they were not so much dissidents as irritants. Gui Minhai and Lee Bo's Mighty Current Media specializes in thinly sourced and often salacious books about the Chinese leadership. At the time the men were kidnapped, the company was said to be planning a book called *Xi Jinping and His Six Women*. One recent book purports to tell how first lady Peng Liyuan lost her virginity. (The Hong Kong Free Press, a nonprofit news Web site started last year, published the following quote from the book: "Peng Liyuan quietly pushed open that half-closed door in the General's Building, like a wisp of soft wind. The house was silent and empty except for one room where light came out, that was Li Hui's bedroom. . . . Before he could finish talking, Peng Liyuan stuffed her sweet soft tongue into his mouth . . .")

Had these books been published elsewhere, the offending publishers might have been swatted away with a defamation suit. But the Communist Party so zealously guards the privacy of the leadership that, on the mainland, information about Xi Jinping is available only from state publishers. Most people do not know even relatively anodyne facts, such as the fact that he was previously married and divorced. So Hong Kong bookstores catering to mainland visitors, especially at the airport, do a brisk business in books about China, the serious as well as the silly.

Gui Minhai, who was abducted from his condo in Thailand, is a naturalized Swedish citizen. He studied poetry at the prestigious Peking University, but later discovered that potboilers about the Chinese leadership were more lucrative. Three months after his disappearance, the state news agency Xinhua released a scripted confession, in which Gui said he had returned to China voluntarily to face charges for a 2003 car accident in which a young woman died. "Returning to the Chinese mainland and surrendering was my personal choice and had nothing to do with anyone else. I should shoulder my responsibility and I don't want any individual or institutions to interfere, or viciously hype up my return," the statement said.

> China's treatment of its critics is notorious. Between July and September of last year, two hundred and eighty human-rights lawyers and activists were detained, according to Human Rights Watch. The extralegal methods used in these recent cases go even further: they are tantamount to kidnappings.

Lee Bo (also known as Paul Lee), a British national, was investigating the disappearance of Gui Minhai and his three other colleagues, and giving interviews pressing for their release, when he himself fell into the dragnet. According to some accounts, he was set up by the person who claimed to be putting in a large book order.

A pro-Beijing legislator at first claimed that Lee had crossed to mainland China to visit a prostitute and was detained there. Last month, that flagrant lie was changed to another, when a fax from Lee appeared, saying he had gone to China voluntarily to "assist in an investigation." The three Mighty Current employees taken into custody within China made similar claims in calls to their families.

Li Xin, the journalist who disappeared in Northern Thailand, apparently was not connected to the others who vanished. He worked as an editor for the Web site of *Southern Metropolis Daily*, which is based in Guangzhou and is part of China's feistiest media group. Li had angered Chinese authorities by exposing the inner workings of the censorship system. According to Radio Free Asia, he had been threatened with espionage charges unless he informed on fellow dissidents. Early last year, Li fled to Thailand, seeking political asylum.

On February 3rd, Li's wife said that she had received a telephone call from her husband in which he told her that he was in Chinese police custody and that he had come back voluntarily. "I felt he was forced to say those words, that he said them against his will," she told the *Guardian*.

Jerome Cohen, a law professor at New York University and an expert on the Chinese legal system, believes the recent round of abductions were so ham-handed that they may have been the work of local authorities, perhaps from Guangdong Province, across the border from Hong Kong. "You have to wonder what level of government authorized this," said Cohen. "This is so embarrassing to the P.R.C." He says the abductions will damage Beijing's efforts to legitimately retrieve criminal suspects, especially those targeted in Xi Jinping's anti-corruption drive, who have fled with their money to the United States, which does not have an extradition treaty with China.

The abductions have only added to the hostility toward the mainland in Hong Kong, which was brought to a standstill in 2014 by tens of thousands of student protesters. Last month, several thousand people marched there to demand the release of the bookstore owners and staff, who have been dubbed the "Bookstore Five." Martin Lee, a lawyer who helped draft Hong Kong's constitution, calls the abductions the "most worrying thing that has happened in Hong Kong since the handover in 1997." In a report issued last Thursday, the British Foreign Office concluded that Lee Bo was "involuntarily removed" from Hong Kong, and for the first time accused China of breaching the treaty that authorized Hong Kong's handover.

The kidnappings in Thailand are especially worrisome to the international community. Thailand is a destination for refugees from all parts of Asia, from the Rohingya of Myanmar to North Koreans. But with Thailand now ruled by a military junta, which took power in 2014, and its economy limping, the country is increasingly bowing to the will of Beijing. In November, it repatriated two pro-democracy activists to China despite the fact that they had papers from the U.N. High Commissioner for Refugees confirming they were to be settled in a third country. In July, Thailand sent home one hundred Uighurs, Muslims from northwestern China who often are denied passports and so try to leave China via land borders without documentation.

The kidnappings bring Thailand's capitulation to a new level. Most countries do not even permit their allies to spirit away whomever they like without at least some veneer of legality. But Thai officials dithered in investigating the disappearances, saying that they could not do anything about the two disappearances unless family members came to Thailand to file missing person reports. When *Time* reporter Hannah Beech toured Gui Minhai's apartment last month—two months after he disappeared but before he was known to be in Chinese custody—she was told that the Thai police had never visited. The wife of Li Xin, the missing journalist, told *Voice of America* that the Thai Police refused to handle the case and instead urged her to contact the Chinese embassy in Bangkok.

Consider, by way of contrast, that after the Central Intelligence Agency snatched Egyptian cleric Hassan Mustafa Osama Nasr off the streets of Milan, in 2003, and transported him out of the country, Italian prosecutors filed kidnapping charges against twenty-three Americans, including the C.I.A. station chief. They were convicted in absentia. Italy is still actively pursuing their extradition.

Chinese Workers Foxconned

By Ross Perlin
Dissent, Spring 2013

The suicide nets are still there. Foxconn, the giant electronics manufacturing sub-contractor, installed them in 2010, a year when fourteen workers died after jumping from the ledges and windows of crowded dormitories. In addition to the wide mesh nets, stretched low over the streets of Foxconn's company towns, the corporation has twenty-four-hour "care centers," "no suicide agreements," and a psychological test to screen out potentially suicidal workers, charged to the job applicant. It has raised wages significantly, but only in the face of runaway inflation, steep hikes in the minimum wage, and mounting worker unrest. Media attention and pressure from Apple, one of its main customers, backed up by a program of regular factory audits, seem to be driving incremental improvements in working conditions.

But the real Foxconn story is unfolding elsewhere. The Taiwan-based firm is rapidly expanding from China's industrialized coast into its vast interior, establishing new production facilities in impoverished provinces such as Henan, Hubei, and Sichuan, far from the labor metropolis of Shenzhen, a dangerous Detroit in the making. Major expansion is also underway in Brazil, India, Mexico, Malaysia, and central Europe, notwithstanding the strong presence of unions in some of those locations. In a dramatic inversion, the company announced late last year that it would soon start manufacturing in the United States itself. Energy costs, access to markets, public relations, and wage stagnation in middle-income labor markets are all part of the equation. The geography of expansion also reflects a global leveling: wages in America's "right-to-work" states, the European periphery, and the BRIC (Brazil, Russia, India, and China) countries are increasingly entering a similar range.

At the same time, the drive to automate is intensifying, with Foxconn CEO Terry Gou promising to have a million robots (dubbed "Foxbots") working the assembly lines within the next few years. Delivering flexibility and scale at rock-bottom prices, Foxconn keeps pounding out the very real underpinnings of the New Economy, remaking global manufacturing in its own image, as did Ford or Toyota in very different times and places. Foxconn stands as the archetypal industrial firm for today's planet of slums.

With some 1.4 million workers in China alone, the company is the world's second-largest private employer after Wal-Mart. Its recent moves to diversify (and fragment) its labor force are a response to several interconnected pressures: rising costs, outside scrutiny, hiring and retention in an increasingly tight Chinese labor market, worker militancy, and surging demand from such customers as Apple and Samsung. Nearly all firms that manufacture for export in China are facing the same challenges and mulling their options. At stake is the Pearl River Delta's thirty-year run as the world's factory floor. The region will doubtless remain an industrial heartland and a crucial labor battleground for years to come, but capital is on the move again.

Designed in California, Assembled in China

Foxconn is disrupting its own model from a position of strength, atop a seemingly impregnable supply chain and flush with record profits. The iPhone and iPad, potent new symbols of globalization, are a far cry from the channel-changing knobs for televisions with which Foxconn started in the 1970s. Gou recognized early on the opportunities opening up across the Taiwan Strait and the lucrative role there for ethnic Chinese investors and entrepreneurs from outside the mainland. When Michael Dell visited Shenzhen in 1995, according to one oft-told tale, Gou offered to introduce him to local officials in return for the chance to drive Dell to the airport. One unscheduled detour to the Foxconn factory later, Gou had landed his first big American client.

The Pacific System, which has its roots in the postwar development of Japan and South Korea, describes an ever-deepening interdependence and a series of dyads: American consumption and Asian labor, American innovation and Asian manufacturing, American debt and Asian savings, American power and Asian acquiescence. In its latest form—the co-evolution of Silicon Valley and China's Special Economic Zones (SEZs), particularly in information technology and alternative energy—it can be summed up in the words, engraved on nearly every Apple product: "Designed by Apple in California, Assembled in China."

The dark double of Apple's Cupertino headquarters in Silicon Valley, where several thousand highly paid engineers "design" gadgets and software, is Foxconn's Longhua facility in the Shenzhen SEZ, where some 300,000 Chinese migrant workers do the assembling. Sometimes called Foxconn City, this immense factory town reportedly turns out 137,000 iPhones a day, or 90 per minute; 300,000 iPad cameras can be assembled in two shifts. Workers may be producing Nintendo video game consoles, Amazon ebook readers, Dell laptops, Nokia phones, or Sony televisions.

The major inland factories, established within the last few years, tend to be more specialized: iPads in Chengdu, iPhones in Zhengzhou, and so on. Salaries are far lower than on the coast, reflecting prevailing and minimum wage rates (China has no national wage floor). Provincial governments have actively courted the company, hoping to jumpstart industrialization. The company is credited with introducing to China the "labor discipline" needed for high-quality precision manufacturing.

The workers are part of China's "floating population" of 200 million migrants, at the bottom of what Taiwanese tech entrepreneur Stan Shih calls "the smiling curve." Controlling the upturned edges of the smile—brand, design and engineering on one side and marketing, sales, and external relations on the other—is what ensures serious value extraction, mega-profits. The curve keeps cropping up, ever more U-shaped, in industry after industry, from commodities such as coffee to complex finished goods. Apple can keep 58.5 percent of an iPhone's sale price, according to a team of academic researchers, while most of the rest goes toward high-end materials and components and 1.8 percent to manufacturers in China, of which only a fraction ends up in the hands of workers. With its razor-thin margins, Foxconn survives by operating at tremendous scale and holding labor costs as close to zero as possible.

Most workers are in their late teens and early twenties, supplementing their family's meager farming incomes and seeking their fortune in the big city. Lacking residence permits, they live apart from the locals and may not have access to basic services. As Ching Kwan Lee writes in *Against the Law: Labor Protests in China's Rustbelt and Sunbelt*, these *nongmin gong* (peasant workers) remain very much distinct from the country's traditional, class-conscious proletariat. They are arguably a labor aristocracy nurtured by Mao Zedong and other Chinese Communist Party (CCP) leaders, particularly at state-owned enterprises in the Northeast. Working mostly at private, export-oriented manufacturers in the Southeast, like Foxconn, the *nongmin gong* aspire to rural entrepreneurship or white-collar work. Their families' experience of Maoism was rural, and they may embrace contingent work. Most stay at Foxconn for less than a year, seeing it as little more than a stop on the way. At Longhua alone, 24,000 workers quit every month, according to the *Guardian*, and large-scale recruitment and hiring are non-stop.

> **Unsafe conditions are pervasive in Chinese factories, and Apple's supply chain has been no exception. An explosion at Riteng, which now produces the iPad Mini, left more than sixty injured, some severely disfigured. The severe poisoning of some 140 workers at Apple supplier Wintek with n-hexane, a chemical used to clean touchscreens, was the first incident that galvanized workers to hold Apple directly accountable, says Crothall.**

The work is tedious, exhausting, high-pressure. "Tasks in the electronics industry are very precise with lots of small details," says Debby Chan Sze Wan of SACOM (Students and Scholars Against Corporate Misbehavior), a Hong Kong-based watchdog. "The main reason leading to unrest is tension in the factory. The structural problem is the production plan set by Apple and Foxconn," she adds, explaining that holiday periods, new product releases, and customer complaints can result in several breakneck months followed by extended downtime.

Collective Stirrings

Specific grievances trigger widening revolts: delayed or miscalculated wages, personal conflict, shock worker quotas, changes in the nature of the work. The only unions are ineffectual branches of the state-controlled All-China Federation of

Trade Unions, although the company announced in early February that genuinely representative union elections would be held, through secret ballot, later this year—an unprecedented move for a large Chinese employer. The results remain to be seen, but this public commitment clearly foregrounds Foxconn's strategy of being seen as a leader on labor issues within China. Both the company and the government are eager for labor peace and "bureaucratized" dissent, channeled from protest actions into grievance procedures.

Wages average from $1 to $2 an hour, including overtime and depending on location. They are attractive only by impoverished rural standards. Fifty-hour work weeks and twelve-hour shifts are typical, but up to one hundred-hour work weeks are not unheard of during peak production. Foxconn has pledged that, as of July 2013, no one will work more than China's legal maximum of forty-nine hours a week—an unprecedented commitment to comply with the law. Workers worry about a drop in their earnings, although the company claims it will make up the difference through raises. Gou fancies himself a latter-day Henry Ford, but he has not introduced any equivalent of the pioneering $5-a-day wage, which put Model Ts in reach of those who built them. Few Foxconn workers can afford the iPads and iPhones they assemble.

In early 2012, 150 protesting workers at Foxconn's Wuhan facility threatened collective suicide from the factory roof. It was a sign of how far things have come since the individual suicides of 2010, but managers and local CCP officials talked them down with promises of improvements. In September, a riot involving several thousand workers broke out at the company's Taiyuan plant, apparently after workers were beaten repeatedly by security guards. Only a week later, under intense pressure to produce newly announced Apple products and conform to ever more stringent standards, up to 4,000 workers at Foxconn's Zhengzhou plants went on strike, according to Li Qiang of the New York-based China Labor Watch.

The workers, mostly from the Onsite Quality Control team, reportedly followed their foremen off the factory floor and succeeded in paralyzing production for the better part of a day. The Taiyuan riot was only ended by the deployment of five thousand police officers. In both cases, Foxconn's characterization of the incidents as mere worker "disputes" was unconvincing—instead, they fit a pattern of increasing worker assertiveness. "At present, all of the disputes we see involve specific grievances about pay, working conditions, and management practice," says Geoffrey Crothall of China Labour Bulletin, a Hong Kong nongovernmental organization. "What is changing is that the workers are better organized and more able and more determined to press for their demands."

As China's largest private employer, Foxconn is more careful than most, but the company has a long rap sheet. Reports have uncovered repeated instances of required, excessive, and unpaid overtime. Management style and training are "military style," says Chan, with talking forbidden on some factory floors and certain forms of corporal punishment, common in China, considered acceptable. Production targets are raised regularly without corresponding wage increases. It is not unusual for workers to be on the production line all but two or three days of a month, ten or eleven days in a row. Many workers live eight to a room in the dorms. "They don't really know or hear what workers want or what workers are demanding," says Li of China Labor Watch.

In 2011, an explosion left four workers dead and eighteen injured at the company's Chengdu plant, which the company had constructed in just seventy-six days. The cause alleged by city officials—a build-up of combustible dust at a workshop for polishing iPads—had been reported by SACOM just weeks earlier and ignored. Unsafe conditions are pervasive in Chinese factories, and Apple's supply chain has been no exception. An explosion at Riteng, which now produces the iPad Mini, left more than sixty injured, some severely disfigured. The severe poisoning of some 140 workers at Apple supplier Wintek with n-hexane, a chemical used to clean touchscreens, was the first incident that galvanized workers to hold Apple directly accountable, says Crothall.

Foxconn's rampant use of students and minors further underlines its pursuit of cheap, flexible labor. When the fallout of the 2010 suicides left Foxconn with a labor shortage, the Henan provincial government, busy wooing the company to set up shop in the province, eagerly stepped into the breach. Giving them only nine days' notice, the province directed 100,000 vocational students to staff the Shenzhen assembly lines as "interns" (the Chinese term shixi can also mean "trainee"). Students who failed to go—there was little in the way of education or training—were told they would not be allowed to graduate.

"Interns" have become a significant component of Foxconn's labor force, constituting as much as 15 percent at peak times, or 180,000 interns company-wide, making it by far the largest "internship" program in the world. Teachers have been stationed in the factory compound to monitor attendance, and some interns have been as young as fourteen—by the company's own admission—in violation of Chinese law. According to SACOM's Chan, Foxconn and other manufacturers that use interns are now doing so "covertly" to avoid detection and culpability, hiring them through the same labor agencies that hire Foxconn's precarious "dispatch workers," who are thus deprived of standard benefits and protections. The casualization of Foxconn's labor army is well underway.

Beyond Foxconn

Beyond better-known facilities such as Foxconn City stretches a vast network of factories whose conditions have remained largely hidden from view. The same is true of most Foxconn and Apple suppliers—indeed, the country's "iEconomy" represents just a fraction of industrial activity and worker activism. So is China "the epicenter of global labor unrest," as Eli Friedman wrote in issue 7/8 of Jacobin? Not yet, but the country's labor movement, under deeply adverse conditions, has a pulse. The China Labour Bulletin tracked nearly four hundred strikes in 2012 alone, as reported in the local media, and the unreported number is surely many times that. All are effectively wildcat strikes, as Friedman points out, since Deng Xiaoping, made wary by the Polish Solidarity movement, revoked the constitutional right to strike in 1982. Today, strikes are not explicitly forbidden, but they do not enjoy the legitimacy, or even tolerant support, that they once elicited, depending on individual circumstances, in the period before Deng's reforms.

Most strikes are short-lived "livelihood struggles," undertaken as just one of many individual or collective strategies of survival and resistance. In this respect, worker activism follows the distinctive Chinese pattern of "mass incidents," a vague, catchall term used by the authorities for any case of civic unrest involving a group of people. Mass incidents vary substantially in nature and in scope—from the outburst of some aggrieved petitioners to a large-scale march—but the overall number is exploding, with one sociologist at Tsinghua University estimating 180,000 in 2010 alone (the last year for which any figures are available).

Few Chinese strikes encompass demands for political reform or unionization—workers understand that this is a bridge too far. The few underground attempts to form independent unions, particularly in the wake of 1989's Beijing Massacre have been summarily suppressed. NGOs and lawyers helping workers through individual struggles have slightly more breathing room. The number of petitions and arbitrated labor disputes has grown exponentially in recent years, as workers learn their rights under the significant 2008 Labor Contract Law. Once a laboratory for runaway capitalism, Shenzhen is now a hotbed of experimentation for labor law and activism. Yet most of the government-run Labor Bureaus responsible for enforcement "are marginalized and play second fiddle to economic and commerce bureaus," writes Ching Kwan Lee.

So what leverage do workers have? China's rapidly aging population, a side-effect of the One-Child Policy first implemented in the late 1970s, promises a tighter labor market for the foreseeable future. And a significant portion of today's *nongmin gong* are "second-generation" factory workers, more likely to constitute a self-aware class-in-the-making. With the industrialization of the interior (by Foxconn and others), workers are now closer to their home villages and may be in a better position to build cultures of solidarity within China's highly fractured ethnic and regional landscape.

Apple's rise to become one of the most recognized and coveted brands in China—from almost complete obscurity even five years ago—may also play a role. When Apple's seventh store in mainland China opened late last year in Shenzhen, it was

> **Westerners convince themselves that such factories are still "opportunities" that "lift people out of poverty". The immiserating forces that created that status quo go unmentioned, as do the tragedies and deceptions that workers face on a daily basis.**

an acknowledgment that the company had come full circle, its future resting as much with China's white-collar consumers as with its industrial workers. What will Chinese consumers demand? "[They] are starting to care about these things," points out Li Qiang, "but the problem is you want to buy a cell phone, you want to make a choice, but there's no choice."

While they leave for more permissive jurisdictions and automate the rest, Apple, Foxconn, and others are also reforming just enough to withstand the attacks. Last year, Apple finally released a list of 156 suppliers and became the first electronics firm to join the industry-funded Fair Labor Association (FLA), a nonprofit that audits factories. The attention of watchdogs such as SACOM and China Labor Watch, as well as two years in the glare of the media spotlight—including a Saturday Night Live skit and the popular, if discredited, stage monologue of the actor Mike Daisey—are also forcing Foxconn into a grudging responsiveness.

Foxconn is singled out "because it's the biggest and the problems are most concentrated," Li says, although it's "not that bad" compared to other Chinese factories. The country's worst labor conditions are almost certainly in the state-run *laogai* (prison labor camps) or at no-name, small- and medium-sized enterprises—illegal coal mines, construction firms, and so on—that fly entirely beneath the radar of the law and watchdog groups. Their products also find their way to the West, as when, in late December 2012, a package of Halloween decorations at Kmart was found to contain a desperate note from a prisoner doing forced industrial labor at Masanjia Labor Camp. The incoming leadership may finally be prepared to dismantle these camps.

The playbook is familiar from the anti-sweatshop movement of the late 1990s and early 2000s. Reporters, campaigners, consumers, shareholders, and watchdog groups find a high-profile target (a Nike or an Apple), galvanize media interest, compile reports, demand transparency and codes of conduct, perform audits, rinse, and repeat. The factory fire that killed 112 garment workers in Bangladesh in late November 2012 highlighted what happens when media attention and public concern wane. Many Westerners convince themselves that such factories are still "opportunities" that "lift people out of poverty" and are preferable to the status quo. The immiserating forces that created that status quo go unmentioned, as do the tragedies and deceptions that workers face on a daily basis. Nor is there always a happy ending a decade or a generation later.

Manufacturers hope to stave off genuine worker power and democracy on the shop floor with a bureaucracy of audits and a veneer of paternalism. "To be honest," says Crothall, "the FLA audits (like all audits) have had minimal impact on workers' actual pay and conditions." Elizabeth Balkan, a former factory auditor who has worked in China, notes that "the FLA standards, answering to many different stakeholders, serve an important, if limited role, in improving supply chain standards. But they are not the most stringent, there are other more stringent standards in the industry." She describes the compliance industry as "a very crowded landscape" full of competing and confusing standards and groups, with the corporations that pay the bills "unwilling or unable to come together with a unified set of standards," given obstacles such as shareholder requirements. Dummy factories and other corrupt and deceptive practices "come up all the time," says Balkan, although "there are real and immediate consequences" if an auditor is directly rebuffed or deceived.

Some thirty thousand factories are audited in China each year, according to Li Qiang. Besides inducing "audit fatigue," writes Alexandra Harney in *The China*

Price, the system helps absolve China's own labor inspectors of responsibility and "doesn't address ever-lengthening supply chains." "Like many industries," says Balkan, "it exists not to make improvements, but because there's a demand for those services." She adds that she started seeing factory flight from coastal China to cheaper areas as early as 2004, and that her later audits were increasingly in places such as Mauritius, Jordan, Sri Lanka, and sub-Saharan Africa, often in Chinese-owned factories staffed by Chinese workers.

Meanwhile the Chinese government is relentlessly pushing the country into post-industrial territory, promoting a consumer-driven economy based on services and innovation. The eagerness to send manufacturing offshore, or at least move it to cheaper areas domestically, matches that of Ronald Reagan's and Margaret Thatcher's governments in the 1980s. After all, if industrialization is just a stage—a brief national adolescence—there won't be time for it to give rise to dangerous social movements. The production lines will keep humming, leaving barely a scratch or a smudge on our touch-screens.

Crackdown in China: Worse and Worse

By Orville Schell

The New York Review of Books, April 21, 2016

"As a liberal, I no longer feel I have a future in China," a prominent Chinese think tank head in the process of moving abroad recently lamented in private. Such refrains are all too familiar these days as educated Chinese professionals express growing alarm over their country's future. Indeed, not since the 1970s when Mao still reigned and the Cultural Revolution still raged has the Chinese leadership been so possessed by Maoist nostalgia and Leninist-style leadership.

As different leaders have come and gone, China specialists overseas have become accustomed to reading Chinese Communist Party (CCP) tea leaves as oscillating cycles of political "relaxation" and "tightening." China has long been a one-party Leninist state with extensive censorship and perhaps the largest secret police establishment in the world. But what has been happening lately in Beijing under the leadership of Chinese Communist Party General Secretary Xi Jinping is no such simple fluctuation. It is a fundamental shift in ideological and organizational direction that is beginning to influence both China's reform agenda and its foreign relations.

At the center of this retrograde trend is Xi's enormously ambitious initiative to purge the Chinese Communist Party of what he calls "tigers and flies," namely corrupt officials and businessmen both high and low. Since it began in 2012, the campaign has already netted more than 160 "tigers" whose rank is above or equivalent to that of the deputy provincial or deputy ministerial level, and more than 1,400 "flies," all lower-level officials.[1] But it has also morphed from an anticorruption drive into a broader neo-Maoist-style mass purge aimed at political rivals and others with differing ideological or political views.

To carry out this mass movement, the Party has mobilized its unique and extensive network of surveillance, security, and secret police in ways that have affected many areas of Chinese life. Media organizations dealing with news and information have been hit particularly hard. Pressured to conform to old Maoist models requiring them to serve as megaphones for the Party, editors and reporters have found themselves increasingly constrained by Central Propaganda Department diktats. Told what they can and cannot cover, they find that the limited freedom they had to report on events has been drastically curtailed.

The consequences of running afoul of government orders have become ever more grave. Last August, for instance, a financial journalist for the weekly business magazine *Caijing* was detained after reporting on government manipulation of China's stock markets and forced to denounce his own coverage in a humiliating self-confession on China Central Television (CCTV). And more recently media outlets were reminded in the most explicit way not to stray from the Party line when Xi himself dropped by the New China News Agency, the *People's Daily*, and CCTV.

"All news media run by the Party [which includes every major media outlet in China] must work to speak for the Party's will and its propositions, and protect the Party's authority and unity," Xi warned. In front of a banner declaring "CCTV's family name is 'the Party,'" Xi urged people who work in the media to "enhance their awareness to align their ideology, political thinking, and deeds to those of the CCP Central Committee." Then, only days later the Ministry of Industry and Information Technology announced new regulations banning all foreign-invested media companies from publishing online in China without government approval.

But the crackdown has hardly been limited to the media. Hundreds of crosses have been ripped from the steeples of Christian churches, entire churches have been demolished, pastors arrested, and their defense lawyers detained and forced to make public confessions. And even as civil society has grown over the past few decades, a constraining new civil society law is now being drafted that promises to put NGOs on notice against collaborating with foreign counterparts or challenging the government.

At the same time, independent-minded researchers at think tanks and outspoken professors at universities worry about the "chilling effect" of Xi's policies on academic life in both China and Hong Kong. Feminist activists demonstrating against sexual harassment have been arrested for "picking quarrels and provoking trouble," while human rights lawyers have been swept up in a mass wave of arrests for "creating public disorder," and even for "subverting state power."

But what has been perhaps most unexpected about this trend is the way that Beijing has begun to extend its claim to control people and organizations beyond its borders. Despite its stubborn defense of the sanctity of sovereignty, its agents have begun reaching overseas to manipulate the foreign dialogue by setting up hundreds of Confucius Institutes, newspapers, magazines, and even TV networks that answer to the Central Propaganda Department and the CCP.

The Chinese government is also denying visas to "unfriendly" (*buyouhao*) foreign journalists and scholars; blocking foreign websites with which it disagrees; demanding that public figures like the Dalai Lama, Hong Kong activists, or Chinese dissidents be refused foreign platforms; threatening the advertising bases of overseas media outlets that challenge its positions; and now even abducting foreign nationals abroad and "renditioning" them back to China where it forces them into making televised confessions. It is hardly surprising that [the] Chinese have started whispering about a new "climate of fear" (*kongbude qifen*), what Eva Pils of King's College London School of Law calls "rule by fear."

What is most striking about these new tactics is their boldness and unrepentant tone. Instead of denying or apologizing for them, the CCP seems to proudly proclaim them as part of a new Chinese model of development, albeit one that has no use for liberal values from the West. In the new world of resurgent Chinese wealth and power, what is valued is strong leadership, short-term stability, and immediate economic growth.

Sitting at the very epicenter of this new nationwide campaign to more tightly control and rejuvenate China through a combination of more muscular leadership, regimented thought, and deeper loyalty to Xi is the Central Commission for Discipline Inspection (CCDI). Long one of the Party's most powerful, secretive, and feared internal organs, the CCDI is dedicated to "maintaining Party discipline." But when Xi came to power and appointed Vice-Premier and Politburo Standing Committee member Wang Qishan as its secretary, he also charged it with launching an unprecedented new anticorruption campaign.

Wang is the "princeling" son-in-law of former Vice-Premier Yao Yilin. The son of a university professor and himself a student of history, he has headed up the China Construction Bank and also creatively handled China's financial and commercial affairs under Hu Jintao when he worked closely with US Secretary of the Treasury Henry Paulson to guide the early years of the Strategic and Economic Dialogue between the US and China. That period is looked back on as a particularly constructive one between the US and China. Why Wang gave up this portfolio to become an anonymous grand inquisitor is unknown, but his friendship with Xi, formed when both were "sent down" (*xiafang*) as youths to the same dirt-poor region of Shaanxi province in the early 1970s, may help explain his willingness.

According to Li Ling of the University of Vienna, who has written about the CCDI, "the party disciplinary system was and remains primarily a means for consolidating the authority of the Party Central Committee and preserving party unity."[2] But since Wang took over in 2012, its already significant network of twelve branch offices have along with the Central Commission expanded their number of investigations from twenty in 2013 to more than a hundred in 2016 to make it one of the most important organs in Xi's effort to bolster China's one-party system. Its work is considered so important that it is even allowed to hire and fire outside the Organization Department, the centralized clearing house that controls other high-level appointments.

As an old-style Leninist party in a modern world, the CCP is confronted by two major challenges: first, how to maintain "ideological discipline" among its almost 89 million members in a globalized world awash with money, international travel, electronically transmitted information, and heretical ideas. Second, how to cleanse itself of its chronic corruption, a blight that Xi has himself described as "a matter of life and death."

The primary reason the Party is so susceptible to graft is that while officials are poorly paid, they do control valuable national assets. So, for example, when property development deals come together involving real estate (all land belongs to the government) and banking (all the major banks also belong to the government), officials vetting the deals find themselves in tempting positions to supplement their paltry salaries by accepting bribes or covertly raking off a percentage of the action. Since success without corruption in China is almost a non sequitur, officials and business-men (and heads of state-owned enterprises are both) are all easily touched by what Chinese call "original sin" (*yuanzui*), namely, some acquaintance with corruption.

Although secret investigations, censorship, and political trials are nothing new in China, what is unique about the CCDI's part in Xi's anticorruption campaign is its explicitly extrajudicial status. The investigations it launches take clear precedence over the judicial processes that police, lawyers, and judges would normally carry out in democratic societies. The CCDI is unencumbered by any such legal nice-ties, except when show trials are needed at the very end of a case so that a formal sentence for, say, corruption, can seem to have been delivered "according to law," a phrase the CCP tirelessly uses as if incantation alone could make it true. But by then, of course, "guilt" has long since been established and all that is usually needed is a little legal theater to give the CCDI's investigation an air of legitimacy.

Besides investigating corruption and violations of "Party discipline," the CCDI has one other more nebulous charge: to "achieve an intimidating effect" on wrong-doing, as its website described it in 2014. In other words, it hopes "by killing a few chickens to frighten the monkeys" (*xiaji jinghou*), as the ancient adage puts it, in hopes of discouraging other potential malefactors. The commission has even launched a new website and smartphone app that allows whistle-blowers to upload incriminating photographs and videos of officials caught violating new sumptuary rules or even *in flagrante delicto*.

As if the CCDI's own investigative arm, the Discipline Inspection Supervision Office (*Jijian jianchashi*), was not up to the ambition of Xi's purge, the Party has now also breathed new life into a second organ, the Central Inspection Patrolling Group (CIPG, *xunshizu*). It was originally set up in 2003 to investigate "leading cadres" whom the CCDI may have shielded owing to its own nepotism and cronyism. With each of their teams headed by a retired ministry-level official and reporting to the Central Committee's new "Central Leadership Inspection Work Leading Group," the CIPG has grown quickly into an important and feared investigatory unit within China's already extensive security apparatus. Although it technically reports directly to the Party Central Committee, like the CCDI, its day-to-day activities are under the command of Wang Qishan, making him the *capo di tutt'i capi* of China's secre-tive investigations units.

When a "tiger or fly" comes under suspicion by either investigative branch, the suspect can be detained for what is called "double designation" (*shuanggui*), mean-ing that they give themselves up for investigation at a designated time and place, but only by the CCDI. Kept in isolation—often under an around-the-clock suicide watch by multiple "accompanying protectors"—there are only murky limitations on the length of time a suspect can be held and no provisions for habeas corpus, legal counsel, or appeal. The object of *shuanggui*, according to the scholar Li Ling, "is to destroy the detainees' psychological defense system so that he or she will 'start to talk.'" Although some reform measures have recently been taken, in the past forced confession and physical abuse, even torture and death, have not been uncommon. Because any investigation comes with strong presumptions of guilt, *shuanggui* is usually as much a verdict as the start of an evidentiary process. Needless to say, few things strike more terror in the hearts of officials than news that they, or their "work unit" (*danwei*), are on the CCDI's hit list.

"The CCDI's anticorruption campaign is chillingly evocative of the draconian repressions launched by the Eastern Depot during the Ming dynasty," one historically minded corporate consultant told me. She was referring to a period in imperial history that represented a high tide of Chinese despotism. As most Chinese know from histories, popular novels, and TV dramas, the Ming dynasty was characterized by factionalism, intrigue, paranoia, intimidation, fratricide, and extrajudicial ruthlessness. Trusting no one and fearing treason everywhere, the Yongle Emperor (reigning 1402–1424) sought to protect the throne with an elaborate network of internal surveillance and espionage.

> **Because [Xi's] policies also grow out of a deeply paranoid view of the democratic world, they make it extremely difficult for China to effectively cooperate with countries like the US on crucial areas of common interests such as antiterrorism, climate change, pandemics, and nuclear proliferation.**

When, like Xi Jinping, the Ming emperor decided that his existing security apparatus, the so-called "Embroidered Guard" (*jinyiwei*), was inadequate to the task of protecting his reign against subversion, he set up the infamous "Eastern Depot" (*dongchang*) and put it under the leadership of loyal palace eunuchs. Here secret files were maintained on all officials, just as today's "dossier" (*dangan*) system keeps files on contemporary Chinese. With its epic history of forced confessions, torture, and grisly assassinations, this Ming dynasty security apparatus became a "diabolical force behind the throne," writes historian Shih-shan Henry Tsai, "a monstrous secret police apparatus" whose "power grew like a giant octopus, extending to every corner of the empire."

However, so rife with paranoia was the Ming court that later emperors came to distrust even the "Eastern Depot" and so set up the "Western Depot" (*xichang*) as well, yet another security organ outside of regular bureaucratic channels. The proliferation of security organizations under Xi Jinping today is hauntingly suggestive of this Ming precursor.

Moving away from the "consensus-style leadership" that came to distinguish China since Mao's repressive rule, Xi Jinping has not only recentralized power, but just as Ming emperors abolished the position of prime minister, he has marginalized the position of the modern-day premier. Instead, he has set up a series of new "leading small groups" (*lingdao xiaozu*) and made himself head of the most important ones (covering such fields as military reorganization, cyberhacking, economic reform, maritime rights, etc.). More than *primus inter pares*, Xi has become what

Party propaganda organs now grandly tout as the "core" (*hexin*) of the Party. As a well-known Chinese cultural figure recently complained in private, "Our leadership now has an indelibly 'dictatorial personality' (*ducaide xingge*)."

As popular as Xi's battle against corruption has been among ordinary people—a 2014 Harvard study showed him as having the highest approval ratings of any world leader—it has had an undeniably chilling effect on anyone hoping to speak truthfully to power. And with its evolution from an anti-corruption drive to a far broader purge of political and ideological rivals, many fear that China is now regressing into a period of neo-Maoism.

Such fears were only reinforced when over the New Year's holiday Xi made a televised pilgrimage to Jinggangshan where Mao had set up his first revolutionary base in 1927. Here Xi was seen paternalistically "at one with the masses," sharing a meal with peasants in front of a reverential poster of Chairman Mao. And his trip has generated a great many photographs, news clips, fawning pop tunes, and videos all extolling the benevolence of "Uncle Xi" (*Xi dada*).

Then in late February, he ordered a yearlong socialist education campaign, especially designed for those comrades who might be experiencing "wavering confidence in communism." He particularly recommended careful study of Mao's 1949 essay "Methods of Work for Party Committees."

The notion that the "Mao Zedong Thought" that had dominated the Cultural Revolution would ever make a comeback in China had long seemed as unlikely as it was unwelcome. But now that China is sliding ineluctably backward into a political climate more reminiscent of Mao Zedong in the 1970s than Deng Xiaoping in the 1980s, more and more educated Chinese are making allusions to such frightening periods of Chinese history as the Cultural Revolution and the Ming dynasty. And more and more of them are also seeking to financially anchor themselves abroad by finding ways to park assets outside their country, making it hardly surprising that China has been hemorrhaging foreign currency, with $1 trillion said to have fled the country last year alone.

When in 1978 the twice-purged Deng returned to power to lay out an ambitious reform agenda that allowed post-Mao China to enjoy greater liberalization in both its economic and political life, there was great relief. And during the relatively tolerant decade that followed, prior to Tiananmen Square in 1989, it was possible to imagine that with the passage of time China would not only become more market-oriented, politically open, and committed to the rule of law, but more in the world. Such optimism was only reinforced by such notions as China's "peaceful rise" propounded later under Hu Jintao.

However, since Xi Jinping's investiture such roseate hopes of a China slowly evolving away from its Leninist past have become increasingly remote. Indeed, in recent weeks, just as China's annual "Two Meetings" (the National People's Congress and the People's Political Consultative Congress) were being held in Beijing, Xi's efforts to command greater Party discipline and to censor the media began to provoke surprising levels of popular protest, including a flurry of unprecedented public challenges to both his policies and authority posted on the Internet. For example, an open letter by New China News Agency reporter Zhou Fang criticized censors for their "crude" and "extreme" violations of online freedom of expression. "Under the crude rule of the Internet control authorities," Zhou wrote, "online expression has been massively suppressed and the public's freedom of expression has been violated to an extreme degree."

Zhou's letter spread like wildfire online before being taken down by censors. Another online letter appeared in the government-linked news site "Watching" (Wujie). It was signed by an anonymous group labeling themselves as "loyal Communist Party members" and not only accused Xi of launching "a cult of personality," but publicly urged him to step down from office. "You do not possess the capabilities to lead the Party and the nation into the future," it declared.

His authoritarian style of leadership at home and belligerent posture abroad are ominous because they make China's chances of being successful in reforming its own economy—on which the entire world now depends—increasingly unlikely. At the same time, because they seem bound to make the Party more dependent on nationalism and xenophobia, Xi's policies also seem destined to prevent Beijing from being able to recast its inflamed relations with its neighbors around the South and East China seas. Finally, because such policies also grow out of a deeply paranoid view of the democratic world, they make it extremely difficult for China to effectively cooperate with countries like the US on crucial areas of common interests such as antiterrorism, climate change, pandemics, and nuclear proliferation.

Whatever may come, China is undergoing a retrograde change that will require every person, business, and country dealing with it to make a radical reassessment of its willingness to seek convergence with the rest of the world.

Notes

1. See Susan Jakes, "Visualizing China's Anti-Corruption Campaign," ChinaFile.com, January 21, 2016.

2. Li Ling, "The Rise of the Discipline and Inspection Commission, 1927–2012: Anticorruption Investigation and Decision-Making in the Chinese Communist Party," *Modern China*, February 16, 2016.

One Year Later, China Still Holding American on Spying Charges

By Jeff Stein
Newsweek Global, March 25, 2016

She had been in and out of China dozens of times over the years. She had led powerful business delegations from her hometown of Houston to Shenzhen, China's Silicon Valley. So nothing seemed out of the ordinary on March 19, 2015, when Sandy Phan-Gillis wrapped up another successful business trip to China with a large group that included Houston's mayor pro tem, Ed Gonzalez.

Over dinner that night, the 55-year-old businesswoman excused herself to meet a friend. The next day, as she stood in line with her group waiting to cross the border into Macau, they suddenly noticed she was gone. They moved on without her. Hours later, she telephoned one of them in Macau. She also called her husband, Jeff Gillis, an oil and gas services manager in Houston. She said she would be staying in China a few more days. Two more days passed before Gillis got another call from his wife. Once again, she said she would be staying in China to wrap up some business. But this time, he later told reporters, her voice sounded strained.

And then another week passed with no word. Frantic, Gillis called the U.S. Consulate in Guangzhou and filled out a missing person's report. Twenty minutes later, an official there called back. Only then, on April 1, did Gillis learn that his wife, a naturalized American originally from Vietnam, was in the custody of Chinese state security. But another six months would pass before Beijing finally explained why: Phan-Gillis was "suspected of engaging in activities that have harmed China's national security," the Foreign Ministry announced. She was "assured of all her rights . . . is in a good state of health and is cooperating with the investigation," it added in a statement.

But an investigation of what? The ministry gave no further details. "They told us that she is accused of stealing state secrets," Phan-Gillis's daughter, Katherine, said after the Foreign Ministry's September 22 statement, breaking the family's six-month silence on the affair. But in the year since she was detained at the border, Chinese officials have not produced evidence of any illegal activity by her. And a year after her arrest, she remains a prisoner in the ancient city of Nanning, 365 miles west of Hong Kong, undergoing constant interrogation. There are no charges, much less a public arraignment and trial, in sight.

"I just thought this had to be a huge mistake," her husband said following the Foreign Ministry statement. "My wife is not a spy; she is not a thief. She is a hard-working businesswoman who spends huge amounts of time on nonprofit activities that benefit Houston-China relations."

Since last September, the family has remained silent. Fearing Chinese reprisals, Gillis said he could not discuss his wife's situation with *Newsweek*. "Families of loved ones in detention centers in China face a dilemma," says John Kamm, a San Francisco businessman who runs a foundation that promotes human rights there. "Should they go public or stay silent? Many fear that by going public the loved one will suffer." But "on balance," Kamm says, speaking out "has proven to be the right decision, but it remains the most difficult, most agonizing decision to make."

Phan-Gillis's family has wrestled with that quandary. After China aired its accusations this past September, the family spoke out and opened a website publicizing their plight. But within a few days, they closed it and stopped giving interviews, with the family's lawyer saying they had "reached a time when it is best to let the State Department and White House negotiate for Sandy, and I am winding down the media campaign."

The State Department says it's following her case closely. Senior U.S. officials, including Deputy Secretary Tony Blinken, "have raised Ms. Phan-Gillis's case with Chinese government officials on multiple occasions," a department spokeswoman, Anna Richey-Allen, tells *Newsweek*. Asked whether Secretary of State John Kerry raised Phan-Gillis's case during his visit to Beijing in January, another department official would say only, on terms of anonymity, "I can assure you that the topic of human rights in China certainly came up." Meanwhile, according to Richey-Allen, U.S. consular officials in Guangzhou, three and a half hours from Nanning by bullet train, have visited Phan-Gillis regularly over the past year, 11 times in all.

"My sense is that State is handling this discreetly and with diligence," says Joseph DeTrani, a top former CIA and State Department expert on China. Making a public ruckus over her case could backfire, he adds by email, "given Beijing's preference for discreet discussions/negotiations."

But Michael Pillsbury, a longtime senior China hand at the Pentagon and on Capitol Hill, argues that "the only way for the American side to succeed" is to get in Beijing's face, "to specifically deny the allegations and to present proof that the charges are false." As for the risk that doing so might prompt Beijing officials to think Phan-Gillis is unusually important to Washington, Pillsbury is dismissive. "Sure, it does raise her value in Chinese eyes," he says, "but what if it were you?"

Theories abound on why China arrested Phan-Gillis. One is that she got wrapped around an axle of Chinese Premier Xi Jinping's so-called "anti-corruption campaign," which has rolled up scores of high officials associated with his predecessors on charges of participating in massive bribery schemes. Last year, the *Houston Chronicle* noted that Phan-Gillis was wired into powerful circles in China: "As president of the Houston Shenzhen Sister City Association and a longtime consultant connecting businesses in southern China with their counterparts in Houston, she knew all kinds of power brokers here and counted many as friends," the paper said. Thus, it's possible Beijing's real interest in Phan-Gillis last year was what she could tell anti-corruption investigators about the business dealings of her Chinese connections, with the spy charges used as a ruse to justify holding her.

Her jailing came as Xi's campaign to revitalize the Chinese Communist Party was cresting on a wave of "enhanced patriotic education," as Robert Daly, director of the Kissinger Institute on China and the United States, recently put it. Chinese state television, with its round-the-clock programming of documentaries and dramas recycling Japanese war crimes, its invective against U.S. and Japanese opposition to Beijing's claims in the South and East China seas and de-

> **In China, there is no "due process" as it's understood in the West. Human rights activists and lawyers are routinely jailed. Recently, anti-regime publishers have been hunted down abroad and rendered to China.**

nunciations of the Obama administration's attacks on Chinese cyberthefts of U.S. government and industrial secrets, made a spy war almost inevitable.

In 2013, the U.S. charged six Chinese nationals with conspiracy to steal specially engineered rice and other seeds allegedly taken from a company in Arkansas. The next year, it indicted five Chinese military officers with the cybertheft of U.S. energy, steel and aluminum companies' secrets, as well as hacking into trade unions. In May 2015, a Chinese professor was arrested and charged with stealing U.S. cell phone technology when he landed at Los Angeles International Airport.

Beijing has responded with several arrests of foreigners on charges of stealing state secrets, including four Japanese, as well as a Canadian missionary couple, Kevin and Julia Garratt, who had lived in China for decades and operated a coffee shop near the North Korean border. In January, a Swedish human rights activist, Peter Dahlin, was held for three weeks on suspicion of endangering national security until he agreed to a staged TV confession that he had broken the law, "caused harm to the Chinese government and hurt the Chinese public," according to the BBC.

In China, there is no "due process" as it's understood in the West. Human rights activists and lawyers are routinely jailed. Recently, anti-regime publishers have been hunted down abroad and rendered to China. Authorities put away suspects and release them when it suits them, and not always on the merits of the case. Kevin Garratt, for example, has been held on charges of spying and stealing state secrets since late January. But his wife's situation is unknown. She spent six months under "residential surveillance" before being released on bail in February 2015, but there has been no news of her status or whereabouts since.

Last September, a weak and frightened Phan-Gillis dictated a letter to her husband through a visiting U.S. consular official. "You don't know this country and how dangerous it is for you," she said. "Please try harder for lobbying and negotiation for my release through Congress and the president." The family's local congressman, U.S. Representative Al Green, a Democrat, did write to Barack Obama. When

Newsweek inquired, his office declined to say what Green asked or how the White House responded.

A swap is not likely, some experts say, until China formally charges Phan-Gillis with espionage—followed by an offer from the U.S. to return one of China's accused spies held here. But if Phan-Gillis is truly innocent, others say, the U.S. would be loath to make such a deal. Yet another, albeit slim, possibility in the minds of some experts would be a deal to get Phan-Gillis back in exchange for a Chinese fugitive in the U.S., such as Yang Xiuzhu, a former senior official now being held in a New Jersey deportation facility, whom Beijing badly wants extradited to stand trial on corruption charges. Since she has applied for political asylum, however, that's not likely.

Asked for comment on the Phan-Gillis case, a spokesperson for the Chinese Embassy in Washington, D.C., says there is no "further information to provide."

Meanwhile, March 19 marks a year since Phan-Gillis was arrested, with no visible movement on her case. And without some sort of deal, she'll probably stay in jail, says influential China-watcher Bill Bishop, publisher of the *Sinocism* newsletter.

"If the U.S. isn't offering up something the Chinese want," he tells *Newsweek*, "why would they release her just because a U.S. official asked?"

China's Race Problem

By Gray Tuttle
Foreign Affairs, May/June 2015

For all the tremendous change China has experienced in recent decades—phenomenal economic growth, improved living standards, and an ascent to great-power status—the country has made little progress when it comes to the treatment of its ethnic minorities, most of whom live in China's sparsely populated frontier regions. This is by no means a new problem. Indeed, one of those regions, Tibet, represents one of the "three Ts"—taboo topics that the Chinese government has long forbidden its citizens to discuss openly. (The other two are Taiwan and the Tiananmen Square uprising of 1989.)

But analyses of China's troubles in Tibet and other areas that are home to large numbers of ethnic minorities often miss a crucial factor. Many observers, especially those outside China, see Beijing's repressive policies toward such places primarily as an example of the central government's authoritarian response to dissent. Framing the situation that way, however, misses the fact that Beijing's hard-line policies are not merely a reflection of the central state's desire to cement its authority over distant territories but also an expression of deep-seated ethnic prejudices and racism at the core of contemporary Chinese society. In that sense, China's difficulties in Tibet and other regions are symptoms of a deeper disease, a social pathology that is hardly ever discussed in China and rarely mentioned even in the West.

When placed next to the challenge of maintaining strong economic growth, fighting endemic corruption, and managing tensions in the South China Sea, China's struggle with the legacy and present-day reality of ethnic and racial prejudice might seem unimportant, a minor concern in the context of the country's rise. In fact, Beijing's inability (or unwillingness) to confront this problem poses a long-term threat to the central state. The existence of deep and broad hostility and discrimination toward Tibetans and other non-Han Chinese citizens will prevent China from easing the intense unrest that roils many areas of the country. And as China grows more prosperous and powerful, the enforced exclusion of the country's ethnic minorities will undermine Beijing's efforts to foster a "harmonious society" and present China as a model to the rest of the world.

It Takes a Nation of Billions to Hold Us Back

Estimates vary, but close to 120 million Chinese citizens do not belong to the majority Han ethnic group. Ethnic minorities such as Kazakhs, Koreans, Mongols, Tibetans, Uighurs, and other groups represent only eight percent of China's population. But their existence belies a commonplace notion of China as a homogeneous society. It's also worth noting that, taken together, the regions of China that are dominated by non-Han people constitute roughly half of China's territory and that if non-Han Chinese citizens formed their own country, it would be the 11th largest in the world, just behind Mexico and just ahead of the Philippines.

Although Tibetans represent only about five percent of China's non-Han citizens, their struggle attracts significant international attention and is in many ways an effective stand-in for the experience of the other minority groups. Tibetans have long been treated as second-class citizens, deprived of basic opportunities, rights, and legal protections that Han Chinese enjoy (albeit in a country where the rule of law is inconsistent at best). The central government consistently denies Tibetans the high degree of autonomy promised to them by the Chinese constitution and by Chinese law. The state is supposed to protect minority groups' cultural traditions and encourage forms of affirmative action to give minorities a leg up in university admissions and the job market. But such protections and benefits are rarely honored. The state's approach toward the Tibetan language well illustrates this pattern: although the government putatively seeks to preserve and respect the Tibetan language, in practice Beijing has sought to marginalize it by insisting that all postprimary education take place in Chinese and by discouraging the use of Tibetan in business and government.

More overt forms of discrimination exist as well, including ethnic profiling. Security and law enforcement personnel frequently single out traveling Tibetans for extra attention and questioning, especially since a wave of protests against Beijing's policies—some of which turned violent—swept Tibet in 2008. Hotels in Chinese cities routinely deny Tibetans accommodations—even those who can "pass" as Han, since their identity cards designate them as Tibetan. Worse, since 2008, the state has placed new restrictions on Tibetans' civil rights, forbidding them to establish associations devoted to issues such as the environment and education—something Han Chinese are allowed to do.

Deprivations of that kind are part of a broader, more systemic inequality that characterizes life for Tibetans in China. Andrew Fischer, an expert on Tibet's economy, has used official Chinese government statistics to demonstrate that Tibetans are much less likely to get good jobs than their Han counterparts due to the lack of educational opportunities available to them. Even in Tibetan-majority areas, where Tibetans should enjoy some advantage, Tibetans earn lower incomes relative to Han Chinese.

It is hard to know exactly what role racism or ethnic prejudice plays in fostering these inequalities. In part, that is because it is difficult to generalize about the views of Han Chinese toward Tibetans and other minorities; just like in the West, public opinion on identity in China is shaped by the ambiguity and imprecision of concepts such as ethnicity and race. Still, it is fair to say that most Han Chinese see Tibetans and other minorities as ethnically different from themselves and perhaps even racially distinct as well.

That was not always the case. In the early twentieth century, Chinese intellectuals and officials talked about Tibetans and Chinese as all belonging to "the yellow race." By the 1950s, however, such ideas had gone out of fashion, and Mao Zedong's government launched a project to categorize the country's myriad self-identifying ethnic groups with the aim of reducing the number of officially recognized minorities—the fewer groups there were, the easier they would be to manage, the government hoped. This had the effect of creating clearer lines between the various groups and also encouraged a paternalistic prejudice toward minorities. Han elites came to see Tibetans and other non-Han people as at best junior partners in the project of Chinese nation building. In the future, most Han elites assumed, such groups would be subsumed by the dominant culture and would cease to exist in any meaningful way; this view was partly the result of Maoist tenets that saw class consciousness as a more powerful force than ethnic solidarity.

Racism with Chinese Characteristics

Perhaps the most striking aspect of contemporary racism and ethnic prejudice in China is its continuity with the past. Throughout the many convulsions China has experienced in the past century, there has never been a watershed moment or turning point in Chinese thinking about race and ethnicity. And regardless of communism's putative colorblindness, racial and ethnic identity was central to early, pre-Maoist versions of Chinese nationalism, which never ceased to influence the country's political culture.

Although traditional Chinese thought posited the superiority of Chinese culture, it was not explicitly racist. But during the late nineteenth and early twentieth centuries, Chinese intellectuals who had studied in Japan—which, during that period, was self-consciously embracing many Western ideas, including some relating to race—began bringing home new, more essentialist ideas about race and ethnicity. Chinese scholars adopted the Japanese term minzoku-shugi (minzu zhuyi in Chinese), which Chinese speakers use today as the equivalent of "nationalism." But as the historian Frank Dikotter has argued, minzu zhuyi "literally meant 'racism,' and expressed a nationalist vision of race."

By the 1920s, the question of China's racial and ethnic identity began to take on greater importance as the revolutionary leader Sun Yat-sen sought to transform the crumbling Chinese empire into a modern state. In 1921, Sun declared that China must rid itself altogether of the idea of separate races. "We must facilitate the dying out of all names of individual peoples inhabiting China, i.e., Manchus, Tibetans, etc.," Sun said. He had a specific model in mind: the United States. "We must follow the example of the United States of America," he said, in order to "satisfy the demands and requirements of all races and unite them in a single cultural and political whole, to constitute a single nation."

Of course, at that time, the United States was hardly a paragon of racial justice and tolerance. But in the decades following Sun's remarks, the U.S. civil rights movement began the process of eliminating legally sanctioned discrimination and reducing prejudice in society. Although racial inequality remains a serious problem in the United States, individual and official views on race have changed dramatically during the past century.

The story is far less hopeful in China. Although China's constitution and ethnic autonomy laws create the appearance of progress, there are no mechanisms for enforcing the vision of equality put forward by those texts. Put simply, there is no Chinese Department of Justice or Chinese Supreme Court to which Tibetans can appeal to fight discriminatory practices.

Minority Report

It is hardly surprising that Han views of Tibetans include an undercurrent of prejudice and paternalism. After all, Tibet came to be ruled by Beijing through conquest.

One of the main challenges facing Mao's Communist forces after their triumph in the Chinese Civil War was the consolidation of the central government's control of China's frontier provinces. Between 1949 and 1951, Chinese Communists used the threat of overwhelming military force to incorporate Tibet into China. By that point, Tibet had enjoyed self-rule, if not international recognition as a state, for more than three decades.

From the beginning, racial nationalism played a crucial role in Beijing's consolidation of control over Tibet. In this respect, Chinese communism mirrored the European colonialism that had dominated China in earlier eras. In 1954, the state formally "recognized" some 30 ethnic groups, including the Tibetans, as minority ethnicities. Over the course of the next three decades, Beijing would add another 18 ethnic groups to that list. Of course, within the borders of their home territories, many of those groups made up almost total majorities.

Beijing spun this recognition as a sign of China's respect for minorities. In reality, it was merely a step in codifying inequality. The Communist Party deemed Tibetans and most other ethnic minorities unfit for leadership roles and made it clear that it was not interested in including them in high-level decision-making. In 1958, authorities placed the leading ethnic Tibetan Communist, Puntsok Wanggyel, under house arrest, charging him with the crime of "local nationalism"; he would spend the next 20 years incarcerated. And although Tibetans and other minority groups were subjected to (and sometimes willingly participated in) the radical reforms and revolutionary violence of the Great Leap Forward and the Cultural Revolution, they were never offered positions within the party leadership.

At the same time, the Communist Party began educating the Han majority in a new form of official racism. Ten "minority films" produced by the government between 1953 and 1966 and screened widely throughout the country depicted ethnic minorities as living in harsh, primitive conditions prior to their "liberation" by Chinese Communists. One of these films, *The Serf* (1963), is still shown today. It features a mute Tibetan protagonist, an unintentionally apt symbol for the way in which authorities in Beijing have sought to silence appeals for Tibetan autonomy and self-representation. Other official efforts to inculcate racist views included museums that distorted Tibet's past, depicting it as a "hell on earth" and portraying Tibetans as a savage, backward people in need of civilizing.

For Mao, instituting an official form of racism was not merely a way to justify quasi-colonial rule in Tibet and elsewhere but also a means for shoring up a Chinese national identity that would otherwise fragment along any number of potential fault lines: rich and poor, urban and rural, coastal and inland. Just as China needed external "others"—the British, the Japanese, the Koreans—to rally against, so the state needed internal others to shift attention away from the party's domination and exploitation of the Chinese people.

Chauvinism or Racism?

The level of tension in Tibet today rivals that of the late 1950s, when the Chinese Communists forced unwelcome social, religious, and economic changes on the area. Early Tibetan attempts to drive out Chinese forces were forcefully suppressed, but Beijing has never been able to totally eradicate resistance to its control. For decades, the Dalai Lama [Lhamo Dondrub] has served as a powerful symbol of Tibetan self-determination—and as an intense irritant to Beijing—traveling the world to garner support for greater political, religious, and civil rights for Tibetans. Meanwhile, challenges to Beijing's control have emerged on the ground as well. During the unrest in 2008, nearly 100 protests broke out in Tibet; around 20 percent of them escalated into violent riots, as protesters looted shops, set fire to police stations and government buildings, and attacked security personnel.

But the 2008 unrest was something of an aberration from the contemporary norm: generally, the central state maintains firm control of the Tibetan Plateau and enforces its rule with a strong military, police, and bureaucratic presence. And rather than produce doubts among the Han majority about the wisdom of Beijing's policies toward Tibet, the unrest instead encouraged some Han Chinese, including well-educated elites, to embrace a belief in an essential racial difference between themselves and Tibetans, whom many Han people have come to see as inherently dangerous.

One reason that attitudes and beliefs about race and ethnicity have changed so little in China is the extent to which the state has blocked discussion of the topic through its control of universities and research institutions and through its obsessive monitoring and censoring of the press and electronic communications. Communist Party ideologues and state media outlets occasionally acknowledge racism by referring euphemistically to "Han chauvinism." But such admissions usually come only in the wake of campaigns to repress dissent in minority-dominated regions.

Occasional criticism from within the Communist Party has had little effect. In a speech delivered in Lhasa, Tibet, in 1980, the party leader Hu Yaobang explicitly compared Beijing's Tibetan policy to colonialism and argued that it had failed to live up to communist ideals: "We have worked nearly 30 years, but the life of Tibetans has not notably improved," he lamented. He called for the state to make good on its promises of autonomy and "to let Tibetans really be the masters of their own lives," proposing a series of specific measures: compelling some Han Chinese officials to learn the Tibetan language, replacing Han party officials in Tibet with ethnic Tibetan ones, and creating more opportunities for higher education in Tibet. But the government mostly ignored Hu's ideas; as with other instances of government recognition of Han chauvinism, this foray into self-criticism was short-lived and inconsequential.

Go West, Young Han

Chinese Communist Party officials have long argued that the government's "Develop the West" campaign, which seeks to increase growth and create economic opportunities in Tibet and other frontier provinces, is the best way to redress ethnic inequality in China. "Development is the foundation of resolving Tibet's problems," declared Chinese President Hu Jintao in 2006. But as Fischer, the expert on Tibet's economy, has revealed, Beijing has directed most of the development funding toward government administration and mas-

> Although China's constitution and ethnic autonomy laws create the appearance of progress, there are no mechanisms for enforcing the vision of equality put forward by those texts. Put simply, there is no Chinese Department of Justice or Chinese Supreme Court to which Tibetans can appeal to fight discriminatory practices.

sive infrastructure projects that surely help central authorities exercise more control but whose benefit to Tibetans is less obvious. Aside from the small number of Tibetans who serve as Communist Party bureaucrats, very few Tibetans can take advantage of such funding and development, since their levels of educational attainment and Chinese-language abilities generally fall below those of the Han workers who arrive from other provinces to compete for jobs. The result is what Fischer has termed "disempowered development," which marginalizes Tibetans in their own autonomous region.

Whatever economic improvements the campaign has created, it has also had a counterproductive effect on Han views of Tibetans. Han people often describe the Tibetans as ungrateful for the largess of the central state. As Emily Yeh, an expert on development in Tibet, has written, many Han Chinese tend to see economic projects there as a "gift" to the Tibetans rather than as an instrument of Beijing's power and control. This perception fuels a view of Tibetans as lazy, unproductive, incapable of managing their own economy, and dependent on the central state.

Making Contact

In the context of the current political environment in China, it is difficult to imagine how the condition of China's ethnic minorities might be improved. The authorities treat any activism or dissent in Tibet and other minority-dominated areas as separatist incitement or even terrorism. And given the fact that Han Chinese citizens themselves enjoy few political or civil rights, it might be unrealistic to hope for an improvement in minority rights.

Still, there are officials within the Chinese Communist Party and state structures who recognize the need for change. One way they could start improving relations among China's ethnic groups would be to revive the ideas of Hu Yaobang. Beijing should increase the numbers of Communist Party and government officials of Tibetan descent; put Tibetans in real positions of power, such as party secretary for the Tibet Autonomous Region; and create a Tibetan-language educational system, especially in rural areas of Tibet. Beijing should also start protecting constitutional guarantees and enforcing existing laws regarding ethnic autonomy, even if doing so requires creating a new administrative or judicial body to hold officials accountable.

Perhaps what China really needs is a truth-and-reconciliation process through which Tibetans and other minorities could safely air their grievances and the Chinese state could acknowledge the abuses of the past. Of course, such an undertaking will be unimaginable as long as China remains a one-party authoritarian state. But nothing currently prevents the Communist Party from simply acknowledging that its policies and practices have failed to bring minority ethnicities willingly into the Chinese state. Such a concession would cost the party very little and would be a significant first step toward improving relations and creating a foundation for a more stable society.

The best hope for change, however, lies with ordinary Han Chinese. If they could see through the Communist Party's attempts to divide and dominate, then they might come to realize that all Chinese citizens share a similar desire for freedom from government oppression. The U.S. civil rights movement succeeded only after significant numbers of white Americans, appalled by the brutality and inequality blacks faced, allied with black organizations and movements that had been fighting against racism for decades. Likewise, any substantive change in Beijing's policies toward Tibetans and other minorities will take a similar change in the views of China's dominant ethnic group.

Such a stark shift might be catalyzed by more person-to-person contact between Han Chinese and Tibetans; according to the so-called contact hypothesis, such interactions make it easier for people from different ethnic groups to overcome their prejudices and fears. Such contact is now happening more than ever before. Owing to the Develop the West campaign, migrant workers now travel to and from Tibet in huge numbers. And since the opening in 2006 of a train line that connects Lhasa to the city of Xining, in Qinghai Province (the first railway to link Tibet to another Chinese region), Han Chinese tourists have poured into the region; this year, 15 million are expected to visit. Meanwhile, even as mainstream Han views of Tibetans have hardened in recent years, a growing number of Han Chinese—especially young people—have begun to demonstrate a sincere and respectful interest in Tibetan society, culture, and religion.

But those developments hardly provide ample grounds for optimism. Barring fundamental changes in Beijing's policies, it is likely that ethnic and racial prejudice against Tibetans and other minorities will remain a serious weakness in the fabric of Chinese society.

4
International Relations and Diplomacy

Feng Li/Getty Images News

Chinese President Xi Jinping accompanies U.S. President Barack Obama to view an honor guard during a welcoming ceremony outside the Great Hall of the People on November 12, 2014 in Beijing, China.

The Balance of Superpowers

The United States and China are two of the world's most powerful nations in terms of both economic strength and military capability. The United States spends 598 billion annually on military development, while China, ranked second, spends 144 billion.[1] By comparison, the next largest military spender is Saudi Arabia, which spends closer to 80 billion each year. The superpowers of the twenty-first century exist in a world where overt military conflict could lead to mutual destruction. Since the development of nuclear weapons technology, military conflict between the world's superpowers has been largely indirect, supporting and funding conflicts in other nations, such as in the Korean War and Vietnam. As the Cold War came to a close with the dissolution of the former Soviet Union and the deterioration of the alliance between China and the Soviet states, the United States has forged tentative, though still problematic diplomatic relationships with its former Cold War enemies. Though diametrically opposed on some ethics and territorial issues, China and the United States have begun to forge, in the 2010s, the first stages of a deeper diplomatic relationship, in spite of the fact that U.S. politicians and the public remain distrustful of China and many consider the nation to be one of the United States' most dangerous potential military rivals. Nevertheless, as diplomatic contact has improved, the United States and China have begun to work together on certain international issues, providing hope of a more stable peace in the future.

Security and Terrorism

In the twenty-first century, both China and the United States have reduced their focus on armaments for large-scale conflicts, while increasing their focus on developing automated weaponry and digital defense technology. Both nations have invested heavily in cyberwarfare technology, the use of computers and digital programming to attack digital systems operated by enemy nations. In the fall of 2015, it was revealed that the Chinese government may have initiated a cyberattack aimed at several U.S.-based security technology companies occurring between 2013 and 2015. The U.S. government warned China about potential reprisal if China engaged in cyberwarfare, while the Chinese government denied responsibility.[2] Though the incident raised tensions between China and the United States, recent dialogues between Chinese and U.S. security agencies suggest possible avenues for future cooperation as both nations are increasingly dependent on digital technology and so vulnerable to "cyberterrorism," or the use of digital weaponry by terrorist organizations. In early 2016, Chinese State Councilor Guo Shenkun met with FBI Director James Comey to discuss the possibility of sharing information on cyberterrorism threats and possible security measures. Though the 2016 meetings are only a first step, both Comey and Guo expressed the hope that such cooperation could lead to a deeper security alliances between the two nations.[3]

Since 2001, the U.S.-led effort to combat international terrorism has been the nation's primary military focus. China has supported the U.S.-led War on Terror, without lending direct military aid to U.S. operations. Many U.S. experts in foreign policy argue, however, that China has used the rubric of anti-terrorism to justify violence and oppression of religious and political organizations with dubious links to terrorist activity. The Chinese government has, for instance, claimed that some Tibetan independence groups are "terrorists," while there has been little evidence to suggest that these organizations have conducted terrorist attacks against the Chinese government.[4]

China's chief terrorist threat comes from the Uighur (Uyghur) ethnic group in the Xinjiang autonomous region of Western China. The Xinjiang region shares borders with Mongolia, Russia, Afghanistan, Pakistan, India, Kazakhstan, Kyrgyzstan, and Tajikistan, and the Chinese government claims that the Uighur independence movement has been supported by Islamic radical groups. A separatist movement began in Xinjiang in the 1990s, with Uighur activists accusing the Chinese government of discrimination and failing to protect the Uighur from racial/religious violence and oppression by China's Han majority. In 2009, a series of violent riots in Urumqi, the capitol of Xinjiang, led to the death of at least 140 Uighur activists and Chinese police.[5] Sporadic clashes between the two groups have continued into 2016. In 2006, U.S. military forces captured a group of Uighur separatists in Afghanistan with reported links to Al-Qaeda.[6] Since then, the U.S. government has recognized some Uighur separatist groups as terrorist organizations. However, U.S. human rights groups have accused China of persecuting all Muslims in Western China under the guise of fighting terrorism.[7]

The most substantive example of U.S.-Chinese cooperation towards global security came in January of 2016, when China, the United States, Pakistan, and Afghanistan joined together to create the Quadrilateral Coordination Group (QCG), an organization dedicated to helping foster the peace process in Afghanistan.[8] Chinese leaders met with leaders in Afghanistan in late January to urge Afghanistan to restart peace talks with the Taliban. As China's Xinjiang region borders Afghanistan, the Chinese government has a vested interest in promoting the peace process, and the nation's role in the newly formed group demonstrates the potential role that China may play in the future of anti-terrorism and global security efforts.[9]

Territorial Expansion and International Security

Another source of tension between the United States and China has been China's territorial expansion in the South China Sea. Between 2013 and 2015, China engaged in a series of construction projects involving building artificial islands in the Spratly Island chain of the South China Sea. The governments of the Philippines, Taiwan, Malaysia, Brunei, and Vietnam also have historical claims to the region and the portion of the ocean that China has developed has long been considered open international territory. China also claims historical ownership of the Spratly Island chain and argues that their development is intended to prevent piracy and to protect their oil and cargo trade. An estimated 40 percent of global shipments pass through the strait, making it an essential region for all oceanic shipping.[10] Since 2013, Chinese and U.S. military vessels have crossed paths in the South China Sea on several occasions, resulting in high-tension standoffs, but no offensive military action.[11] The U.S. military claims that Spratly Island Chain lies in open international waters according to the United Nations Convention on Law of the Sea.

Political analysts have compared the South China Sea issue to the territorial dispute surrounding the Balkan Islands at the beginning of World War II. Though there has been no overt military action, the United States has claimed that it will not allow China to violate United Nations law by claiming exclusive rights to the region. In September of 2015, Chinese president Xi Jinping publically announced that his government would not "militarize" the Spratly Island facilities, though government statements were unclear on how the government defines the "militarization" process.[12]

Even as tensions have risen over China's controversial oceanic expansion, 2015 also marked the first time in history that the U.S. and Chinese military agreed to conduct a series of military-to-military exchanges in an effort to practice working together on humanitarian military operations. Eighty Chinese soldiers visited the Joint Base Lewis-McChord in the first of 11 planned exchanges in 2015–2016, while U.S. solders were invited to visit China's Guangzhou Military Region for another series of simulated disaster relief exercises that same year.[13] While the first exchanges are more of a diplomatic overture, military leaders on both sides expressed optimism that such experiments could lead to more military cooperation moving forward.

A New Era of Diplomacy

While the United States has been slowly building a diplomatic relationship with China since the 1980s, there has been an increase in governmental contact between the two nations in the 2010s as China has emerged as the United States' chief military and economic competitor. Writing in *The Diplomat*, Graham Webster argued that while the U.S. press continues to highlight U.S.-China tensions, the past decade has also seen unprecedented levels of transparency between the two nations.[14] In 2014, the United States and China agreed to relax short-term visas for tourists, students, and travelers, and, as a result, 2015 saw a significant increase in tourist and business travel between the two nations.[15] While the United States continues to oppose China on certain key issues, China's emergence as one of the world's most powerful nations also makes China an important player in the ongoing effort to maintain international security. Political analysts have argued that China played a key role in brokering the Iran nuclear deal in 2015 and that the United States needs China's assistance in efforts to prevent nuclear arms proliferation in North Korea. As China's presence on the world stage increases, therefore, the nation may be in the process of transitioning from the United States' biggest rivals for global power, to one of the nation's most promising future allies.

Micah L. Issitt

Recommended Reading

Ashton, Adam. "U.S. and Chinese Troops Connect in First-Ever Exchange at JBLM." *The News Tribune*. The McClatchy Company. Nov 20 2015. Web. 20 Apr 2016.

Blake, Andrew. "China Urges FBI to Strenghen Cybersecurity, Counterterrorism Cooperation with Beijing." *Washington Times*. The Washington Times, LLC. Mar 15 2016. Web. 20 Apr 2016.

Borger, Julian and Tom Phillips. "How China's Artificial Islands Led to Tension in the South China Sea." *The Guardian*. Guardian News and Media. Oct 27 2015. Web. 20 Apr 2016.

Branigan, Tania. "Ethnic Violence in China Leaves 140 Dead." *The Guardian*. Guardian News and Media. Jul 6 2009. Web. 26 Apr 2016.

Brownlee, Lisa. "China-based Cyber Attacks on US Military are 'Advanced, Persistent and Ongoing': Report." *Forbes*. Forbes, Inc. Sep 17 2015. Web. 26 Apr 2016.

Crawford, Jamie. "U.S. Protests after Chinese Military Jet Lands on South China Sea Island." *CNN*. Cable News Network. Apr 19 2016. Web. 20 Apr 2016.

Denyer, Simon. "China's War on Terror Becomes All-Out Attack on Islam in Xinjiang." *The Washington Post*. Nash Holdings. Sep 19 2014. Web. 20 Apr 2016.

French, Howard W. "China's Dangerous Game." *The Atlantic*. Atlantic Monthly Group. Nov 2014. Web. 20 Apr 2016.

Hunt, Katie. "China to Narrow Gap with U.S. by Increasing Military Spending." *CNN*. Cable News Network. Mar 5 2015. Web. 26 Apr 2016.

"Joint Press Release of the Quadrilateral Coordination Group on Afghan Peace and Reconciliation." *State*. U.S. Department of State. Jan 11 2016. Web. 20 Apr 2016.

Page, Jeremy, Lee, Carol E., and Gordon Lubold. "China's President Pledges No Militarization in Disputed Islands." *The Wall Street Journal*. Dow Jones & Company. Sep 25. 2015. Web. 20 Apr 2016.

Small, Andrew, Wei, Zhu, and Eric Hundman. "Is China a Credible Partner in Fighting Terror?" *Foreign Policy*. The FP Group. Nov 24, 2015. Web. 26 Apr 2016.

"The United States and China to Extend Visas for Short-term Business Travelers, Tourists, and Students." *State*. U.S. Department of State. Nov 10 2014. Web. 20 Apr 2016.

Webster, Graham. "2015: The Year US-China Relations Went Public." *The Diplomat*. Trans-Asia, Inc. Dec 23 2015. Web. 20 Apr 2016.

"Why Is There Tension Between China and the Uighurs?" *BBC News*. Sep 26 2014. Web. 20 Apr 2016.

Wong, Edward. "China Urging Afghanistant to Restart Peace Talks With Taliban." *New York Times*. New York Times Company. Jan 27 2016. Web. 20 Apr 2016.

Notes

1. Hunt, "China to Narrow Gap with U.S. by Increasing Military Spending."

2. Brownlee, "China-based Cyber Attacks on US Military are 'Advanced, Persistent, and Ongoing': Report."

3. Blake, "China Urges FBI to Strengthen Cybersecurity, Counterterrorism Cooperation with Beijing."

4. Small, Zhu, and Hundman, "Is China a Credible Partner in Fighting Terror?"

5. Branigan, "Ethnic Violence in China Leaves 140 Dead."

6. "Why Is There Tension Between China and the Uighurs?" *BBC News*.

7. Denyer, "China's War on Terror Becomes All-Out Attack on Islam in Xinjiang."

8. "Joint Press Release of the Quadrilateral Coordination Group on Afghan Peace and Reconciliation," *US Department of State*.

9. Wong, "China Urging Afghanistan to Restart Peace Talks with Taliban."

10. French, "China's Dangerous Game."

11. Borger and Phillips, "How China's Artificial Islands Led to Tension in the South China Sea."

12. Page, Lee, and Lubold, "China's President Pledges No Militarization in Disputed Islands."

13. Ashton, "U.S. and Chinese Troops Connect in First-Ever Exchange at JBLM."

14. Webster, "2015: The Year US-China Relations Went Public."

15. "The United States and China to Extend Visas for Short-term Business Travelers, Tourists, and Students," *State*.

China Passes Antiterrorism Law That Critics Fear May Overreach

By Chris Buckley

The New York Times, December 27, 2015

China's legislature approved an antiterrorism law on Sunday after months of international controversy, including criticism from human rights groups, business lobbies and President Obama.

Critics had said that the draft version of the law used a recklessly broad definition of terrorism, gave the government new censorship powers and authorized state access to sensitive commercial data.

The government argued that the measures were needed to prevent terrorist attacks. Opponents countered that the new powers could be abused to monitor peaceful citizens and steal technological secrets.

In the end, the approved law published by state media dropped demands in the draft version that would have required Internet companies and other technology suppliers to hand over encryption codes and other sensitive data for official vetting before they went into use.

But the law still requires that companies hand over technical information and help with decryption when the police or state security agents demand it for investigating or preventing terrorist cases.

Telecommunication and Internet service providers "shall provide technical interfaces, decryption and other technical support and assistance to public security and state security agencies when they are following the law to avert and investigate terrorist activities," says the law.

"Not only in China, but also in many places internationally, growing numbers of terrorists are using the Internet to promote and incite terrorism, and are using the Internet to organize, plan and carry out terrorist acts," an official, Li Shouwei, said at a news conference in Beijing.

The approval by the legislature, which is controlled by the Communist Party, came as Beijing has become increasingly jittery about antigovernment violence, especially in the ethnically divided region of Xinjiang in western China, where members of the Uighur minority have been at growing odds with the authorities.

Chinese leaders have ordered security forces to be on alert against a possible terrorist attack of the kind that devastated Paris in November.

Over the weekend, the shopping neighborhood of Sanlitun in Beijing was under reinforced guard by People's Armed Police troops after several foreign embassies, including that of the United States, warned that there were heightened security risks there around Christmas.

In addition, the Chinese Ministry of Foreign Affairs said on Saturday that it would expel a French journalist, Ursula Gauthier, for a report that suggested the Chinese government's unyielding policies were stoking violence by Uighurs in Xinjiang.

Uighurs are a Turkic ethnic minority, largely Sunni Muslim, who have become ever more discontented with controls on their religion and culture and with an influx into Xinjiang of ethnic Han migrants. The government says that violent acts by disaffected Uighurs have been inspired and instigated by international extremist groups, but critics say the conflict arises from homegrown disaffection.

In March of last year, Uighur assailants used knives to slash to death 29 people at a train station in Kunming, a city in southwest China. Last month, the government in Xinjiang said Chinese security forces had killed 28 people who were accused of orchestrating an attack on a coal mine that killed 16 people.

Human rights groups have warned that the law will give even more intrusive powers to the Chinese government, which already has broad, virtually unchecked authority to monitor and detain citizens and to demand information from companies and Internet services.

"While the Chinese authorities do have a legitimate duty in safeguarding their citizens from violent attacks, passing this law will have some negative repercussions for human rights," said William Nee, a researcher on China for Amnesty International who is based in Hong Kong, via email.

"Essentially, this law could give the authorities even more tools in censoring unwelcome information and crafting their own narrative in how the 'war on terror' is being waged," Mr. Nee said.

International companies that use encrypted technology in China had been worried by provisions in the draft law that would have required them to hand over code and other information so that the authorities could monitor users. The law could affect multinational companies like Cisco, IBM and Apple, all of which have big stakes in China.

"These companies have been dealing with this increased, let's call it oversight, for the last two or three years," said Scott D. Livingston, a lawyer who works for Simone IP Services, a consulting firm in Hong Kong, and who has followed the discussions over the law. With the antiterrorism law, Mr. Livingston said, "from the government's perspective, you have a

Critics had said that the draft version of the law used a recklessly broad definition of terrorism, gave the government new censorship powers and authorized state access to sensitive commercial data.

stronger basis to request this access."

In January, foreign business groups wrote to President Xi Jinping to voice collective unease about China's Internet policies, including the draft legislation, which could have required handing over sensitive data and commercial secrets.

In an interview with Reuters in early March, Mr. Obama criticized the proposed legislation and similar initiatives by the Chinese government, and warned that technology companies would not go along with the intrusive demands laid out in the draft law.

A few days before the antiterrorism law passed, Hong Lei, a spokesman for China's Ministry of Foreign Affairs, said at a regular news briefing that criticism from the Obama administration was unfounded.

Mr. Li, the criminal law expert with the National People's Congress, insisted that the new law was no reason for multinationals to be alarmed. "These rules will not affect the ordinary business activities of the firms concerned," he said.

What Does 2016 Hold for China-U.S. Relations in Cyberspace?

By Franz-Stefan Gady
China US Focus, January 29, 2016

Sino-U.S. relations in cyberspace in 2016 will be defined by three key policies: attribution, sanctions, and norms. The first two tacks will be used by the United States to contain malicious Chinese activities in cyberspace (and to assuage the U.S. private sector and U.S. public opinion), whereas the last device will be used for promoting strategic stability between both nations by deepening the understanding of what is acceptable behavior in the cyber realm.

First, while it is true that attribution, i.e., tracing a cyber attack back to its originator, remains difficult, it is not impossible. Both the U.S. government and the private sector have repeatedly called out Chinese hackers in so-called "naming and shaming" campaigns. This tactic consists of either leaking classified intelligence to the press or publishing cyber attack reports by U.S. cyber security firms (which over the years became a clever marketing ploy for those companies). And while "naming and shaming" sustained a severe setback with the Snowden revelations, we will certainly witness a number of such cyber attack disclosures in 2016. However, the shock value—and as a consequence its potential negative impact on the Sino-U.S. bilateral relationship—will be less severe than in 2014 and 2015, given that, after the recent Office of Personal Management data breach and the Snowden disclosures, the threshold for disclosures with the potential to severely undermine the Sino-U.S. bilateral relationship has substantially risen. At the same time "naming and shaming" will at least contain both sides from going overboard when it comes to cyber espionage activities and aggressive network intrusions.

Second, sanctions, while an imperfect tool, appear to have caught the attention of the Chinese leadership in 2015 and will likely play a role in Sino-U.S. relations in 2016 as well. On April 1, 2015, U.S. President Barack Obama signed Executive Order 13694, which argues that "the increasing prevalence and severity of malicious cyber enabled activities originating from, or directed by persons located, in whole or in substantial part, outside the United States constitute an unusual and extraordinary threat to the national security, foreign policy, and economy of the United States."

As a consequence, the Obama White House threatened China with economic sanctions and individual Chinese citizens with travel restrictions should Beijing not rein in its hacker community. One indication that this worked has been the arrest of a number of Chinese hackers prior to the September 2015 state visit by Chinese President Xi Jinping, although there is considerable debate among experts whether there is a genuine connection between the two events. However, the threat of

> **The last quarter of 2015 saw some progress on the diplomatic front in improving relations between the United States and China in the field of cyber security.**

economic sanctions will have significantly higher impact on the senior Chinese leadership in 2016, primarily due to China's deteriorating economic situation, but also due to the international humiliation the country would suffer from being the first nation subject to economic sanctions for cyber attacks.

Third, norms of behavior in cyberspace will gain increasing importance in 2016 and some progress can be expected. For example, in November 2015, the G20 countries, including the United States, China, Brazil and India agreed that international law, including the United Nations Charter, applies to the behavior of nations in cyberspace. (A U.N. Group of Government Experts came to the same non-binding resolution in 2013.) Furthermore, the G20 countries agreed that no country should conduct or support the cyber enabled theft of intellectual property. The U.N. Group of Government Experts also laid out a set of norms and confidence building measures in 2015. These recent developments could serve as additional incentives for both the United States and China to expand these measures.

However, Sino-U.S. disagreement over what constitutes use of force in cyberspace will likely persist. For one thing it is in China's interest to keep the definition vague, since no international norm for retaliation against cyber attacks could then be established, making it more difficult for the United States and its allies to come up with a common response to future state-sponsored malicious cyber activities.

Furthermore, as one scholar told me in an email exchange: "China simply does not pursue these legal concepts for armed hostilities involving cyberspace in the same forensic, semi-obsessive manner as Western scholars and officials." However, some scholars have argued that China sees itself bound by international law, including non-use of force except in self-defense and that this norm is seen to be applying in cyberspace, which is not too different from U.S. and Western positions.

However, we will have to be realistic with expectations in 2016. The United States and China will continue to disagree over internet governance—the former preferring a "multi-stakeholder" position, the latter, a state-centric "multilateral" approach. Chinese state-sponsored cyber attacks against the U.S. private sector will continue most likely at a higher level than in 2015. Both countries will continue to prepare for the possibility of a cyber war, which necessitates probing each other's national critical information infrastructure, and will continue to disagree over China's new anti-terror law, which has the potential to undermine private sector cooperation on combating cybercrime in both countries.

Sino-U.S. Cyber Diplomacy in 2015: A Review

The last quarter of 2015 saw some progress on the diplomatic front in improving relations between the United States and China in the field of cyber security. During a state visit to the United States in September 2015, Chinese President's Xi Jinping and U.S. President Barack Obama agreed to deepen bilateral cooperation and build trust between the two countries in cyberspace by, among other things, refraining from conducting or knowingly supporting commercial cyber-espionage, promoting appropriate norms of state behavior in cyberspace, and establishing a high-level joint dialogue mechanism on fighting cybercrime and related issues.

Indeed, the first meeting of the U.S.-China High-Level Joint Dialogue on Cybercrime and Related Issues took place on December 1, in Washington D.C. in which the participants, including representatives from various U.S. and Chinese departments and ministries, agreed to a set of guidelines for requesting assistance on cybercrime and how to respond to requests; developed the scope, goals and procedures for a joint hotline mechanism; decided to conduct a tabletop exercise involving network protection scenarios in order to deepen the understanding regarding the other side's authorities, processes, and procedures; agreed to further develop case cooperation on cybercrime including the theft of trade secrets; and most importantly agreed to meet again in June 2016. (The U.S.-China Joint Liaison Group on Law Enforcement Cooperation, which has been in existence since the late 1990s, has also monitored bilateral cybercrime issues including child pornography.)

China and the United States, despite some quiet contact between the two governments, have not officially discussed cyber security since May 2014. China at that time suspended participation in the U.S.-China Cyber Working Group after the U.S. Justice Department had indicted five members of the People's Liberation Army for malicious activities in cyberspace. The agreements reached at the December 1 High-Level Dialogue are a notable achievement and should be cause for wary optimism when it comes to the future of Sino-U.S. relations in cyberspace in 2016, although it goes without saying that the agreements have to first be implemented to have any real impact. Nevertheless, the meeting indicated a more conciliatory stance by both countries towards one another's positions on a number of contentious cyber related issues (e.g., the theft of trade secrets), and, more importantly, laid the political groundwork for deeper technical cooperation.

In 2015, the United States and China also stepped up the cyber arms race. In May of last year, China issued its first ever "Military Strategy" emphasizing the importance of cyberspace for future military operations. In 2015, the Pentagon issued a new "Cyber Strategy," and Cyber Command issued a new planning document, titled "Beyond the Build." In addition, the Pentagon issued a new Law of War Manual, in which the pre-emplacement of "logic bombs" in an adversary country's networks and information systems is advocated.

On the more positive side, unless there will be a significant deterioration of relations between both countries (e.g., a military confrontation in the South China Sea), it is highly unlikely that either the United States or China will employ strategic cyber weapons in 2016 to disrupt each other's command and control systems and hack into the software of advanced weapons platforms in order to disable them, since this would be tantamount to a declaration of war.

Eye on Africa: US and China Tussle for Economic Influence

By Yvan Yenda Ilunga
The Conversation, **February 25, 2015**

The US and China are increasingly rivals on the world stage, competing over resources, policy and influence. One region where China has spent years establishing a foothold is Africa. Now the US is also keen to reassert itself after years of economic neglect.

The US fired the latest salvo late last year when it pledged to provide at least $14 billion in public and private assistance in areas such as clean energy, energy, aviation and banking. President Barack Obama told leaders of 50 African countries attending the US-Africa Leaders Summit that Coca-Cola will provide clean water, General Electric will assist with infrastructure development, and Marriott will build more hotels.

But there was a catch, as always. The governments who receive the investments must do more to bolster the rule of law, reform regulations and root out corruption.

That's a key difference between the US and China in their approaches to Africa and elsewhere. The US likes to attach strings, the Chinese just want to do business. And that's why China's economic footprint in Africa dwarfs that of the US. Indeed, it surpassed the US as the continent's largest trading partner in 2009.

About $200 billion of goods and services flowed between China and Africa in 2013, double the $85 billion in trade the US had with the continent.

Africa still offers promise to both superpowers, one waxing, one waning, as a region not yet fully developed but boasting many fast-growing economies. In their pursuit of economic gain, the US and China eye Africa as a fertile land of opportunity. As they race to establish economic control on the continent, it is important to carefully examine the strategies they're employing.

While their economic goals are similar, their terms of engagement are diametrically opposed.

China's Model: Investment Without Meddling

China's strategy in Africa diverges from the traditional model exemplified by the World Bank and International Monetary Fund. That model, which has regulated the principles underlying international investment and trade for decades, aims to establish accountability and ethics at the center of economic cooperation. Critics contend this model is too Western-centric.

China utilizes a "doing business" model that ostensibly treats African states as equal partners and steers clear of their internal affairs—a strategy that appeals to countries used to Western colonies and dictates.

It's built on three strategies that China has used successfully to achieve its African trade goals: flexibility, focusing on infrastructure and cementing partnerships with small businesses.

Flexibility. China invests in Africa with a high degree of flexibility and pays little heed to the existence (or nonexistence) of credible financial institutions, contrary to the norm of American and European investment. Instead, its sole focus is on gaining access to natural resources such as copper and gold, with no interest in building up African institutions.

While this approach draws criticism for its lack of accountability, China has managed to seduce many African governments such as Angola and the Democratic Republic of the Congo with the notion of an equal partnership without internal meddling.

Infrastructure. China has long been Africa's top infrastructure partner. New roads, bridges, hydroelectric dams, schools and hospitals are going up across the country as a result, bolstering economic growth. This hasn't been without criticism: many question the long-term viability of the structures being built and the fact that Chinese workers are imported to do most of the work. Thus while buildings and bridges may rise, few jobs are directly created.

Small business. Lastly, small business owners in Africa and their Chinese counterparts have established strong ties, particularly in clothing and construction. Trade in these sectors has exploded. Yet again, the rapidity with which these partnerships have developed has created some unease among consumers and analysts. The quality of the Chinese products being imported is often low and comes with no warranty or other guarantee.

Despite the problems and criticisms, these three strategies exemplify why the Chinese model has been successful in Africa.

The US Model: Building Strong Institutions

The US has a long history of engagement in Africa, particularly in terms of aid and political and military influence—the case of Rwanda since 1994 exemplifies this. In recent years the U.S. has been shifting toward building economic ties with the continent.

That's now accelerating as developing countries such as China and Brazil dominate growth in the global economy, prompting the Obama administration to launch the US-Africa partnership. Previous efforts were bilateral, this new framework has truly continental ambitions.

The US strategy boils down to building strong institutions and focusing on macro projects.

State building. The main thrust of US investment has long been made through development agencies and financial institutions such as the World Bank and IMF, following the traditional model promoted through structural adjustment mechanisms which focuses on poverty reduction, institutional reforms and free market with highly macro-economic focus in its implementation.

With many countries on the continent still in the process of state-building such as the Democratic Republic of Congo and Central Africa Republic, the US focus on institutional reforms and accountability as a precondition of aid should be encouraged. This approach not only facilitates monitoring and management of the funds distributed. It also helps establish a less corrupt economic space for private enterprise. That, in turn, attracts other foreign investors and makes the state more sustainable.

Based on my personal experience, however, this strategy isn't well received by Africans, who regard it as another symbol of an unequal partnership, with the US imposing its conditions. This inflexible and sometimes overbearing approach sometimes brings more frustration than interest in cooperation.

Big projects. The second US strategy of targeting macro projects in energy, mining and other sectors also often falls flat. The rationale behind making such investments is valid but the idea that the benefits will trickle down has

> **China's strategy in Africa diverges from the traditional model exemplified by the World Bank and International Monetary Fund.**

failed to bear fruit. The promotion of economic growth in Africa requires the creation of a stronger middle class, which in turn requires more small- and medium-sized businesses.

On this, China gets it right. The US will need to reconsider this focus and do more to deal with Africans at the micro level if it wants to establish a long and lasting presence there.

Additionally, the US tendency to interfere in the political affairs of many countries in Africa—such as Libya—gets in the way of cooperation.

Economic cooperation needs to be based on mutual trust, and this is only possible if the US is less forceful in its terms of partnership. Unless the US becomes more flexible, it is unlikely to rival China as Africa's top partner.

Everyone Can Win

Both the Chinese and the American terms of engagement in Africa may be strategically and ideologically valid and justifiable. There are strengths and weaknesses to both approaches.

China's flexibility in contracts and everything else creates a fast win-win situation but does not promote good governance or state building, both of which are sorely needed in Africa.

The US focus on the need for institutional reforms is important, but without a more flexible and adaptive approach this will not work.

As the US shows a growing economic interest in Africa, a key question will be whether the Obama administration can establish a stronger partnership that focuses on business ties and not military force.

Just as China can learn from the US emphasis on state building, the Americans should take a page from the Chinese playbook. The end result would be truly a win-win for everyone.

The Asia-Pacific Cooperation Agenda: Moving from Regional Cooperation Toward Global Leadership

By Charles E. Morrison

AsiaPacific Issues, October 2014

APEC Achievements and Challenges

APEC celebrates its twenty-fifth anniversary in a vastly changed region and world. Since 1989, there has been dramatic economic growth in most Asian developing countries, especially China; regional integration through a combination of reduced political and regulatory barriers and the rise of supply and production chains; and a proliferation of regional institutions and freer trade and investment arrangements. In a context where there is also rising demand that institutions of all kinds, including international organizations, demonstrate concrete outcomes, some would question whether APEC can claim any responsibility for the region's achievements.

In fact, it is very difficult to link APEC as an organization in any specific way to these outcomes. Even the reduction in trade barriers has less to do with Bogor Goals than obligations undertaken as part of WTO commitments, other negotiations, or unilaterally. However, APEC has been part and parcel of the positive changes that have been occurring in the region, and undoubtedly the fact that first ministers, then leaders were meeting on a regular basis provided a positive atmosphere for international interaction and integration. Prior to APEC, there were no such meetings; regional cooperation was nonexistent or confined to subregional or highly specialized organizations with no sense of broad and converging regional interests; and Asia-Pacific engagement in global issues was fragmented and incoherent.[1]

APEC's achievements are much more visible to foreign and trade ministry bureaucracies than they are to the public, or even to more politically and policy aware stakeholders. APEC has proved to be an efficient venue for the leaders of the region to meet. It has helped build some common sense of international economic norms and values and strengthened adherence to the international trade system. It has provided a vehicle for economies with once limited awareness of the WTO system to better understand the rules, obligations, and benefits of the system. While APEC, as a venue for voluntary, nonbinding cooperation, has not itself been a formal vehicle for negotiating free trade areas, much of the inspiration for such agreements has been associated with the APEC process. Freer trade and investment liberalization have been APEC goals for two decades. Today virtually all the economies in the region are engaged in one or another of the major free trade negotiations—the Trans-Pacific Partnership, the Regional Comprehensive Economic Partnership, and the Pacific Alliance. APEC itself may not be a rule-making organization, but it has both deepened adherence to global norms and rules and inspired more liberal trade rule-making at the subregional or plurilateral levels.

APEC no longer remains the only broad-gauged trans-Pacific organization; it has been joined by the East Asia Summit (EAS), which includes the United States as a member. If we consider APEC and EAS as complementary institutions in a broad trans-Pacific cooperation and integration process, this process faces two critical challenges during the coming decades: Will it effectively generate international cooperation among the region's economies in addressing the many continuing and often deepening challenges of the region? And, perhaps even more significantly, can the Asia-Pacific region assume a leadership role in the global system?

A Global Century With an Asia-Pacific Core

East, Southeast, and South Asia, with a little more than half the world's population, are rapidly regaining an equivalent share of world gross product for the first time in two centuries. There are many reasons to believe that despite cyclical variability and a longer-term decline in the growth rates of the more advanced nations associated with the end of catch-up development and demographic aging, the comparative rise of Asia within the global system will continue. Human capital enhancements, increased economic integration, technological leapfrogging, and the growth of middle classes are among the reasons. Projections by the US National Intelligence Council suggest that by mid-century, China will have slightly surpassed the United States as the world's most powerful nation, based on a composite index of the many elements of power.[2] But while the power and influence of China and India will continue to rise, and thus Asia's systemic weight increase, no single country will be as influential in the international system of the future as the United States has been in the last part of the preceding century.

The rise of Asia has led to speculation about an "Asian century." With a continuing diffusion of power, the coming century is much more likely to be a global one. However, the international system will have a trans-Pacific core area with much of the economic power and the potential to provide global leadership for the further development of international norms, rules, and cooperation. In this sense, we may be able to refer to an "Asia-Pacific century."

Defining Questions

Contemplating an Asia-Pacific century, two questions arise: Is North America, with a relatively small share of global population, and a declining share (less than 25 percent by 2050) of global world product, still relevant? Will the nations on the two sides of the Pacific really be able to use their power effectively to assume global leadership? The answer to the first of these is "yes," and to the second, "it depends."

North America's role is not simply based on its population or economic size, but also on the creative dynamism of the American societies, which are constantly being refreshed by new immigration and a highly entrepreneurial culture facilitated by a unique interplay between business, government, and academic sectors, typified by Silicon Valley. Far from retreating from their historical origins as international "melting pots," the United States and Canada remain open to high and increasingly diversified levels of immigration, drawing from human talent pools all over the world. The foreign born in the United States today is estimated at about 46 million of its 318 million people, the highest share for this country in over a century.[3] Canada has an even higher proportion of foreign born, with more than 7 million in a population of 35.5 million. While helping the United States to remain a global center for higher education, advanced research, and cutting-edge technologies, immigrant communities also inhibit retreat toward "isolationism." The United States is likely to continue to provide a leading share of the world's public goods, especially in such areas as international security, disaster relief, and financial systems.

The second question of whether the Asia-Pacific region will step up to global leadership depends on a number of factors and deserves more attention. It may be likely, but there is no guarantee. To be an effective core leadership area, the region needs to meet a number of requirements.

First, the economies need to be stable and secure units, capable of engaging in cooperation and adhering to international commitments. This appears positive. Despite many challenges, the quality of governance continues to improve in most of the region. Second, there need to be harmonious, cooperative international relations among the societies of the region and intergovernmental institutions capable of creating common values, norms, and action agendas. This is currently questionable. The region's global role will be limited if territorial disputes persist, diverting resources and attention from major regional and global issues and challenges. Only by building a sense of community within the Asia Pacific can the region become a truly effective force for global peace- and order-building. Third, there needs to be a continual process of integration and growing connectivity. This has been occurring and is a key objective of the APEC process. The major economies of Asia are now more integrated in terms of trade flows than those of North America, and almost as much as those of the European Union. Continuing this process, as well as improving the interconnectedness of the region in transportation and communication, is an important force for continued Asia-Pacific growth. Fourth, the economies of the region need to be inclusive domestically, drawing upon the whole of the resources of their own societies. APEC's goal of "inclusive" growth is important in this regard, as well as in contributing to the first goal of a "stable and secure unit." Fifth, the APEC economies need to be inclusive internationally, that is, take into account the sensitivities and interests of nations outside the region. Finally, the region will need intellectual, policy, and educational hubs for creative policy ideas and regionally and globally focused leadership training. Just as an integrating Europe required individuals grounded in their own nationalities but with a European sense of challenges and opportunities, the Asia-Pacific region will require such individuals with broad regional and global knowledge.

This last requirement should be a major objective of APEC's working agenda on education. APEC economies can learn lessons from each other's experiences, a main current theme of this work, but they should also strive to build networks of individuals with a similar understanding of regional and global history, challenges, and desirable pathways to address issues. This will be facilitated by the greater mobility of students, joint venture and multinational educational programs, and a truly regional center for Asia-Pacific leadership education.

The Mega-Agenda for APEC

What then are the challenges facing APEC in its twenty-fifth year? The focus here is on the longer-term regional challenges most relevant to an emerging global agenda.

The first challenge, and an essential requirement for all else, is to strengthen the international cooperative relations of the region. This requires overcoming issues of history and focusing on issues of common concern to the APEC community as a whole. In the past, APEC and other regional bodies have been used to dampen regional tensions and reassure populations that leaders remain engaged. But in recent years, leaders have not made such use of APEC and this may have contributed to regional misunderstandings and tension.

Second, there are architectural questions, both within the Asia-Pacific region and between this region and other regional systems and the global system. There is no particular reason that any institution, including APEC, needs to survive in its current form or with its current name. What is important over the longer term is that the process of Asia-Pacific cooperation and economic integration continue. The current architecture of institutionalized regional cooperation with its different components remains a work in progress. The relationship between the East Asia Summit, with its ASEAN base and politico-security dimension, and APEC, with its socioeconomic agenda, will need to be sorted out. Fragmentation into separate processes, however temporarily necessary, undermines political attention and commitment. Moreover, the subregional building blocks of cooperation will need to be filled in. While healthy cooperation takes place in Southeast Asia, Oceania, and the Americas, regional cooperation in Northeast Asia and the North Pacific is quite limited.

> The international system will have a trans-Pacific core area with much of the economic power and the potential to provide global leadership for the further development of international norms, rules, and cooperation. In this sense, we may be able to refer to an "Asia-Pacific century."

Third, APEC should enlarge its stakeholder community within the APEC economies and demonstrate more forcefully its relevance and benefits for the economies as a whole. For the most part, knowledge of and interest in APEC has been confined to bureaucracies. Most of the nongovernmental outreach has been directed toward segments of the business community, as illustrated by the existence of only one advisory committee, the APEC Business Advisory Council. While the business community is an essential sector to be served through APEC, regional integration processes need parallel structures involving parliamentarians and even local political figures, as well as NGOs. Although such involvement does take place, it is usually in settings peripheral to the "core business" of APEC.

Fourth, it is clear that parts of Asia and the Pacific are in the forefront of some of the world's biggest demographic, environmental, and health challenges. If there are models of cooperation in APEC in these areas, they will quite naturally propel the Asia-Pacific region into global leadership roles. Northeast Asia, for example, has some of the world's lowest fertility rates, and Japan and possibly Russia already have shrinking populations. Urbanization is at very high levels or occurring at very high rates in many of the APEC economies. Integrating new citizens into urban communities, providing robust and equitable services, and retaining vitality in rural areas are significant issues not only in themselves, but also to the overall well-being of societies and the quality of their international relationships. With its dense populations and rapidly changing diets and lifestyles, Asia is also at the forefront of many health and environmental challenges. While the medical aspects of these are best dealt with in other forums, general health policies are a legitimate and important topic for APEC cooperation. Sustainable resource use and the environmental agenda for all of the economies have become very acute issues, as attested by the urgent attention the Chinese leadership has vowed to give clean air and water, but the Asia-Pacific regional cooperation agenda in these areas remains underdeveloped. Finally, as mentioned above, APEC should give much greater attention to its education agenda, particularly addressing the task of how to prepare the people of the region for a twenty-first century economy and for global leadership.

Political Champions

Strengthened cooperation in APEC and global leadership from the Asia-Pacific region will, in the end, be driven primarily by the quality, imagination, and attentiveness of political leadership, especially in the larger economies. Without such leadership, modes of cooperation tend to become routinized and bureaucratized, and progress to become incremental. Unfortunately, today's leaders are often highly distracted by the increasingly complex task of domestic governance, combined with responsive rather than proactive approaches to foreign policy issues. But we have a number of new regional leaders who may look upon APEC and the broader regional integration process with fresh eyes. Perhaps this new team of regional leaders can help to formulate a new and workable Asia-Pacific dream.

Notes

1. Charles E. Morrison, "Four Adjectives Become a Noun: APEC and the Future of Asia-Pacific Cooperation," in APEC at 20: Recall, Reflect, Remake, eds. K. Kesavapany and Hank Lim (Singapore: Institute of Southeast Asian Studies, 2009), 30.
2. US National Intelligence Council, "Global Trends 2030: Alternative Worlds," Washington, DC, December 2012.
3. United Nations, Department of Economic and Social Affairs, "Trends in International Migrant Stock: The 2013 Revision," http://esa.un.org/unmigration/TIMSA2013/migrantstocks2013.htm.

Obama's Quiet Nuclear Deal With China Raises Proliferation Concerns

By Steven Mufson
The Washington Post, May 10, 2015

It seemed like a typical day for President Barack Obama. He taped a TV interview on trade, hosted the champion Nascar stock car racing team on the South Lawn, and met the defense secretary in the Oval Office.

Not so typical was something that didn't appear on the public schedule: notification to Congress that he intends to renew a nuclear cooperation agreement with China. The deal would allow Beijing to buy more US-designed reactors and pursue a facility or the technology to reprocess plutonium from spent fuel. China would also be able to buy reactor coolant technology that experts say could be adapted to make its submarines quieter and harder to detect.

The formal notice's unheralded release on April 21 reflected the administration's anxiety that it might alarm members of Congress and nonproliferation experts who fear China's growing naval power—and the possibility of nuclear technology falling into the hands of third parties with nefarious intentions.

Now, however, Congress is turning its attention to the agreement. The Senate foreign relations committee was set to hear from five Obama officials in a closed-door meeting on Monday to weigh the commercial, political, and security implications of extending the accord. The private session permitted discussion of a classified addendum from the director of national intelligence analyzing China's nuclear export control system and what Obama's notification called its "interactions with other countries of proliferation concern".

The White House's willingness to push ahead with the nuclear accord with Beijing illustrates the evolving relationship between the world's two largest powers, which, while eyeing each other with mutual suspicion and competitiveness, also view each other as vital economic and strategic global partners. The Nuclear Energy Institute, an industry trade group, argues that the agreement will clear the way for US companies to sell dozens of nuclear reactors to China, the biggest nuclear power market in the world.

Yet the new version of the nuclear accord – known as a 123 agreement under the Atomic Energy Act of 1954 – would give China leeway to buy US nuclear energy technology at a sensitive moment: the Obama administration has been trying to rally support among lawmakers and the public for a deal that would restrict Iran's nuclear program—a deal negotiated with China's support. Administration officials say the negotiations over the 123 agreement persuaded China to go a "long way" and agree to controls on technology and materials that are tighter than those in the current accord.

Congress can vote to block the agreement, but if it takes no action during a review period, the agreement goes into effect.

If Congress rejects the deal, "that would allow another country with lower levels of proliferation controls to step in and fill that void," said a senior administration official, who spoke on the condition of anonymity so he could talk more freely. "We go into it with eyes wide open," he added. "Without it, we would be less able to press the Chinese to do better on this front."

Although the current nuclear agreement with China does not expire until the end of the year, the administration had to give Congress notice with 90 legislative days left on the clock. Obama also hopes to seal a global climate deal in December featuring China—less than three weeks before the current nuclear accord expires.

Congress isn't convinced yet.

"We are just beginning what will be a robust review process," Senate foreign relations committee chairman Bob Corker said in an email. "These agreements can be valuable tools for furthering US interests, but they must support, not undermine, our nation's critical nonproliferation objectives."

A Quieter Submarine

Henry Sokolski, executive director of the Nonproliferation Policy Education Center, has been urging lawmakers to insist on requiring advance consent for the acquisition by China of a plutonium-reprocessing plant capable of producing weapons-grade material. He also opposes the sale of nuclear energy technologies, especially coolant pumps and high-quality valves known as squib valves, with possible naval use.

Charlotte-based Curtiss-Wright developed advanced coolant pumps for the US navy's submarines. The same plant produces a scaled-up version for the Westinghouse AP1000 series reactors, each of which uses four big pumps. These pumps reduce noises that would make a submarine easier to detect.

That has become a bigger concern since China occupied and started building what looks like a military base on strategic (and disputed) reefs in the South China Sea.

An Obama administration official said the reactor coolant pumps are much too big to fit into a submarine. However, a 2008 paper by two former nuclear submarine officers working on threat reduction said that "the reverse engineering would likely be difficult" but added that "certainly, the Chinese have already reversed engineered very complex imported technology in the aerospace and nuclear fields."

Sokolski thinks the choice between reactor sales and tighter controls is a clear one. "Since when does employment trump national security?" he asked rhetorically.

The US has bilateral 123 agreements with 22 countries, plus Taiwan, for the peaceful use of nuclear power. Some countries that do not have such agreements, including Saudi Arabia, Jordan and Malaysia, have expressed interest in clearing obstacles to building nuclear reactors.

China and the US reached a nuclear cooperation pact in 1985, before China agreed to safeguards with the International Atomic Energy Agency (IAEA). The safeguards went into force in 1989, but Congress imposed new restrictions after the Chinese government's June 1989 crackdown on protesters in Tiananmen Square. The 123 agreement finally went into effect in

> **"If China right now is the great hope for the future of nuclear energy, soon it will be a major reactor exporter to the extent there's a market . . . . So it's a proliferation concern, and it's also a nuclear terrorism concern. The more plutonium there is lying around, the more likely it is that someone will steal it."**

March 1998; President Bill Clinton waived the 1989 sanctions after China pledged to end assistance to Pakistan's nuclear weapons program and nuclear cooperation with Iran.

In December 2006, Westinghouse Electric—majority-owned by Toshiba—signed an agreement to sell its AP1000 reactors to China. Four are under construction, six more are planned, and the company hopes to sell 30 others, according to an April report from the Congressional Research Service.

When it comes to nuclear weapons proliferation, China is in a different category from other 123 agreement nations. It first tested a nuclear weapon in 1964 and now has an arsenal of about 250 nuclear warheads. So US concerns have focused more on whether China has transferred technology to other countries.

"Concerns persist about Chinese willingness as well as ability to detect and prevent illicit transfers," the CRS report said. "Missile proliferation from Chinese entities is a continuing concern." The US wants China to refrain from selling missiles capable of carrying nuclear weapons, a payload of 499kg, as far as 305km. A State Department compliance report in 2014 said that Chinese entities continued to supply missile programs in "countries of concern".

Reprocessing Plutonium

Reprocessing is another key issue.

China has a pilot plant engaged in reprocessing in Jiu Quan, a remote desert town in Gansu province. Satellite photos show that it is next to a former military reprocessing plant, according to Frank von Hippel, a Princeton University physics professor who specializes in nuclear arms control. There is not even any fencing between the sites, he says. "That's been one of the hang-ups of the (reprocessing) deal" that China has been trying to negotiate with France for several years, von Hippel said.

Sokolski said the agreement proposed by Obama lacks a requirement for explicit, case-by-case US permission for a reprocessing project using American technology or material from US reactors. It gives consent in advance. And he fears that over the 30-year life of the new 123 agreement, China might want to compete with Russian and US arsenals and make more bombs, for which plutonium is the optimal material.

Other weapons experts note that China already has enough surplus highly en-riched uranium and plutonium to make hundreds of new bombs. China has indi-cated that it is interested in reprocessing so it can use plutonium as part of the fuel mix in civilian nuclear power plants. And it must offer the IAEA access.

Von Hippel is still concerned. "So if China right now is the great hope for the future of nuclear energy, soon it will be a major reactor exporter to the extent there's a market," he said. "So it's a proliferation concern, and it's also a nuclear terrorism concern. The more plutonium there is lying around, the more likely it is that some-one will steal it."

But the most politically sensitive issue in Congress might turn out to be du-al-use applications of nuclear reactor parts. The latest appropriations bill issued by House armed services committee chairman Mac Thornberry last month would require an intelligence assessment of whether there was "minimal risk" that ci-vilian nuclear technology would be diverted to any "foreign state's nuclear naval propulsion program."

Representative Brad Sherman said that the bill "doesn't mention China by name, though I can't think of another country for which it would be more applicable." He said: "I would be reluctant to approve a 123 agreement unless I knew that the indi-vidual contracts would be properly reviewed."

A Senate armed services committee aide, who was not authorized to speak on behalf of the committee members and commented on the condition of anonym-ity, said the Senate would also focus on military applications of reactor technology for submarines, given rising concern about China's aggressive posture in the South China Sea.

Senator John McCain, chairman of the committee, would not comment for this article, but he has recently questioned continuing engagement with China while it maintains an aggressive approach to regional issues. Last year he opposed a pro-posed visit by a US aircraft carrier to a Chinese port; later, defense secretary Ashton Carter said it would not take place. McCain also said it was a mistake to invite China to the 2016 international maritime military exercise in the Pacific known as RIMPAC.

The senior Obama administration official warned that "if we were not to com-plete an agreement or if restrictions were so onerous, then a lot of the work we've done to bring China into the mainstream and understand the programs they're pur-suing would be lost, and meanwhile our commercial interests would also be hurt."

But the armed services committee aide said: "This is not simply renewing a past agreement. The senators are going to address it in new strategic circumstances."

Too Much History: Can the U.S. and China Look Forward?

By Evan Osnos
The New Yorker, February 14, 2014

History was interrupted on the morning of April 1, 2001, when an American EP-3E reconnaissance plane, carrying a crew of twenty-four, was flying over international waters about seventy miles off the Chinese coast. A Chinese jet approached; it collided with the American plane's propeller and crashed to the sea. The Chinese pilot was killed. The damaged American plane dropped eight thousand feet in thirty seconds before its pilot regained control and made an emergency landing on the tropical Chinese island of Hainan. The crewmembers made a brief, unsuccessful effort to disable the intelligence equipment before the EP-3E was boarded and they were placed under arrest.

President George W. Bush demanded the release of the crew. But Chinese President Jiang Zemin called on Washington to apologize for the incident. It was Bush's first international crisis—a standoff with the first major power to rise since the Cold War. Observers declared that the Sino-American rivalry would be the defining geopolitical challenge of the Bush Presidency. And then, five months later, Al Qaeda attacked the World Trade Center. The United States was pulled into the Middle East and Afghanistan, and the purported face-off with China was paused like a movie mid-scene. (After eleven days on the island, the crew was returned. The Chinese military reverse-engineered the plane's NSA-designed operating system, forcing the Navy to scrap it, which cost hundreds of millions of dollars.)

In the thirteen years since then, the United States poured between four and six trillion dollars into prosecuting wars abroad while China, largely insulated from the conflicts of the day, more than quadrupled its military spending and advanced its claims to territories in the neighboring seas. For years, China maintained a low profile in foreign affairs, something Deng Xiaoping had ordained in his admonition to *taoguang yanghui*—"bide your time, and hide your strength." Douglas Paal, of the Carnegie Endowment for International Peace, wrote not long ago, "You may have missed the funeral, but China's new leadership has quietly buried" that idea. The competition that was postponed in 2001 has never seemed closer at hand, and the U.S. faces a more complex challenge than simply curtailing the rise of a rival.

Secretary of State John Kerry is in Beijing, to meet with senior Chinese officials and make a deceptively simple demand: halt a series of increasingly assertive steps in territorial disputes with its neighbors. The short-term goal is to reduce pressure on Japan and the Philippines, which have clashed with China over contested sections of the East China and South China Seas. But both sides recognize that the long-term goal—to defuse an increasingly tense relationship between the world's two most powerful countries and remove the gathering cloud of a history that neither side can afford to repeat—could hardly be more important.

In the years since that first round on Hainan Island, China has improved its hand. In 2009, China claimed a historic right to control nearly ninety per cent of the South China Sea; in a standoff in 2012, it compelled the Philippines to cede disputed territory. In an interview with the *Times* earlier this month, President Benigno Aquino appealed for international support, comparing this moment to the West's failure to support Czechoslovakia against Hitler's territorial demands in 1938. In a similarly grim comparison, Japanese Prime Minister Shinzo Abe, whose country has been locked in a dispute with Beijing over islands, compared the growing tension to that of England and Germany on the eve of

> **In its dealings with China today, the U.S. confronts a paradox unlike any other it has faced: America is entwined with the People's Republic in ways it never was with prewar Germany or the Soviet Union. Last year, a million and a half Chinese tourists visited America, and two million Americans went to China. The two countries are on pace to become each other's largest trading partners by 2022, and they are actively courting investment from either side.**

the First World War, a century ago this summer. Not to be outdone, a Chinese banker told a Davos audience that the Japanese are the "Nazis of Asia." There are so many casual analogies flying back and forth that the historians Alexis Dudden and Jeffrey Wasserstrom have warned, "Profaning history to begin a new war is simple madness."

Bit by bit, so steadily that it is easy to mistake it for routine sniping, the United States and China are being drawn into what the journalist Geoff Dyer, in a new book, calls "the contest of the century." Most recently, the U.S. has laid new markers on the table to make clear that it will not allow China to alter the distribution of power in Asia—that the U.S., in effect, will meet action with action. In a series of recent statements, American officials for the first time said explicitly that the U.S. believes China's claim to the South China Sea is inconsistent with international law, and that any Chinese attempt to claim a right to air defense in that area would be reflected in the "our presence and military posture in the region."

If these seem like ambivalent actions, they are. In its dealings with China today, the U.S. confronts a paradox unlike any other it has faced: America is entwined with the People's Republic in ways it never was with prewar Germany or the Soviet Union. Last year, a million and a half Chinese tourists visited America, and two million Americans went to China. The two countries are on pace to become each other's largest trading partners by 2022, and they are actively courting investment from either side. The U.S. needs China's involvement on a wide range of priorities, from bringing North Korea back to nuclear-disarmament talks to climate change, Syria, and Iran. (After meeting with Chinese President Xi Jinping and other officials, Kerry sounded encouraged by Beijing's commitment to pressuring North Korea—"China could not have more forcefully reiterated its commitment to that goal"—but he had little progress to report on the territorial disputes.)

At the same time, the United States has reasonably concluded that it cannot afford to ignore the pleas of its allies in Asia or allow an incremental drift toward a more volatile state of play. And so, the U.S. is left to perform a delicate balancing act. It must appeal to what Dyer calls "globalization China"—investment, trade, and engagement—while attempting to police the ambitions of "great power China." That is an ungainly diplomatic dance, but it is the one we've arrived at. Above all, this should be regarded as a moment unto itself, for which analogies to the past are limited in their utility. "History as weaponry," as Dudden and Wasserstrom put it, can cause self-inflicted wounds.

Suspected Are the Peacemakers

By Alex Perry
Newsweek, October 16, 2015

Will China's increased commitment to the U.N.'s troubled humanitarian forces be a blessing or a curse?

China used to disdain the U.N. For three decades after it joined the Security Council in 1971, it mostly didn't even bother to vote on whether to approve peacekeeping missions, which it viewed as interference in the sovereign affairs of others. So when President Xi Jinping announced at the U.N. General Assembly session on September 28 that China would overhaul global peacekeeping with 8,000 extra troops and hundreds of millions of dollars in new funding, he not only upstaged President Barack Obama, who was holding his own peacekeeping summit across town at the time, but signaled a new Chinese attitude toward international intervention. Rather than just oppose it, China now wants to remake it.

Xi announced China would set up a 10-year, $1 billion fund for the U.N.'s work in peace and development, create a permanent, 8,000-strong Chinese peacekeeping quick-reaction force and give $100 million of military assistance to the African Union over five years so the union can create its own crisis intervention force. At a stroke, by adding those 8,000 troops to the 3,000 peacekeepers it already contributes, China became the world's biggest provider of peacekeepers. (The U.S. remains peacekeeping's biggest funder but supplies just 82 soldiers.)

Xi added that he expects China's bigger role to grant it greater influence over peacekeeping and all humanitarian intervention. No longer should the "big, strong and rich . . . bully the small, weak and poor," said Xi. "Those who adopt a highhanded approach of using force will find they are only lifting a rock to drop on their own feet."

Many fans of peacekeeping welcomed China's initiative. Gareth Evans, a former Australian foreign minister who was instrumental in formulating and building acceptance for the Responsibility to Protect (R2P)—the U.N. principle under which all humanitarian military interventions operate—says China's initiative was "wholly appropriate" to the multilateralism that peacekeeping is meant to embody.

Skeptics, however, noted that while China now stresses international consensus, it has recently been acting aggressively in its own neighborhood. It is currently involved in tense disputes over strategic islands in the South China Sea with Japan, the Philippines, Brunei, Vietnam and Taiwan, and is in something of a conventional arms race with the United States. A particular concern prompted by Xi's speech was his emphasis on Africa. The Chinese president said Beijing "firmly supports developing countries' greater representation and influence, especially African countries, in international governance."

To some, this sounded more like self-interest than altruism. As well as being the location for nine of the U.N.'s 16 peacekeeping missions, Africa is where China now has tens of billions of dollars invested in commodities and infrastructure. Keeping the peace in places where China has put its money raises the possibility that Chinese peacekeepers might see their role as protecting things as much as people.

Then again, maybe a little self-interest is exactly what U.N. peacekeeping requires. The history of peacekeeping is littered with failures in places where the famous blue-helmeted forces have no stake in the conflicts they are meant to be keeping a lid on. Take, for example, the world's biggest peacekeeping operation, the U.N. mission in Congo (MONUSCO). Its nadir, and the lowest point for all U.N. peacekeeping, came in November 2012 in Goma, Congo's main eastern city. Equipped with tanks, helicopters, planes, armored personnel carriers and an annual budget of $1.3 billion, MONUSCO's 20,000 men were facing off against 1,000 rebels armed with Kalashnikovs, rocket-propelled grenades and a few ancient tanks and artillery pieces.

When a rebel tank fired a single shell into Goma, the U.N. took decisive action. It fled. The peacekeepers abandoned the civilians they were mandated to protect and retreated to their bases or left the city altogether. The rebels, called the M23, took Goma without firing a further shot. By evening, crowds were gathering in front of U.N. bases, demanding that those peacekeepers who had not already left do so immediately. "You could not defend us," they shouted. "You are useless. You are dismissed."

Looking on in dismay was Alan Doss, head of MONUSCO from 2007 to 2010 and today executive director of the Kofi Annan Foundation in Geneva. "I just don't know if there was a rationale," he now says of that retreat. "I couldn't explain it." On the ground at the time, a Uruguayan U.N. officer told a *Newsweek* correspondent that the reason for the U.N.'s timidity was simple. "I have

> In New York, Xi made clear that China's object was to ensure that poorer, less powerful countries, especially African ones, were no longer subject to the whims of others but, instead, could reassert authority over their own affairs.

a wife and a son back home," he said. "My men have families too. I want us to get out there, but it's not safe. I have to make the right decision for everyone concerned."

The officer was expressing the grand flaw in peacekeeping's noble design: Soldiers sent from one side of the world to the other to protect people they do not know and whose troubles do not interest them typically find themselves undermotivated.

For Uruguayans in Congo, "everyone concerned" did not include the Congolese the peacekeepers were meant to protect.

The U.N.'s repeated peacekeeping failures—this year the U.N. has been unable to prevent massacres in South Sudan and the Central African Republic—prompted U.N. Secretary-General Ban Kimoon to request a sweeping review of the organization's peacekeeping missions, which is ongoing, and Obama to call his summit in New York. But whereas the U.N. and the U.S. initiatives were designed to drum up more resources—and in that they have been successful—China's is aimed at refashioning the whole practice of legal international military action.

Since 2005, humanitarian military intervention has been officially governed by R2P. Supporters of R2P argue that there are universal standards of human rights every government and international governmental body is required to uphold. R2P formalizes that by obligating the international community to override any country's sovereignty by intervening militarily—imposing a no-fly zone, perhaps, or a blockade, bombing campaign or even a ground invasion—if that country is unable or unwilling to stop human rights violations on its territory.

Critics, including the Chinese government, say the universalism to which R2P aspires is a mirage. They point out there are no commonly accepted standards of human rights even within countries, citing differing attitudes about the death penalty in neighboring American states. Better, say the critics, to respect a diversity of opinion. "No civilization is superior to others," said Xi in New York at the U.N. "Each civilization represents the unique vision and contribution of its people."

And in practice, argues China, R2P has been used to impose the views of powerful nations on others. It was used as justification for interventions that include NATO's attack on the forces of Muammar el-Qaddafi in Libya in 2011 and Russia's military actions in Georgia in 2008 and Ukraine in 2014. In this context, if U.N. peacekeeping played a role in this version of R2P, until now it has mostly been a subservient, ex post facto one, mopping up after the primary intervention by a major power, or a bellicose neighbor, is over.

China appears to be trying to reverse that. In New York, Xi made clear that China's object was to ensure that poorer, less powerful countries, especially African ones, were no longer subject to the whims of others but, instead, could reassert authority over their own affairs. The vehicle China has chosen for this pushback is peacekeeping and, in particular, China's funding of a permanent African Union international intervention force.

A model for that force already exists in the form of AMISOM, an African peacekeeping body in Somalia that practices a brand of peacekeeping very different from the U.N.'s. It is also more efficient: Even though it has 22,000 soldiers, more than MONUSCO, AMISOM costs a fraction of a U.N. mission—just $95 million a year, less than a 10th of the annual MONUSCO price tag. And although it operates under a U.N. mandate, AMISOM's commanders—mainly Ugandans, but also Burundians, Ethiopians, Kenyans, Djiboutians, Sierra Leoneans and Ghanaians—interpret that authority much more aggressively. As the Ugandans in the Somali capital of Mogadishu candidly admit, they do not just try to keep the peace. Rather, they impose it by killing anyone making war, in particular fighters from the Al-Qaeda-allied Al-Shabab group.

AMISOM has been largely successful. Where the U.N. and the U.S. failed for two decades, AMISOM has killed thousands of Al-Shabab guerrillas and driven them out of Mogadishu. As a result, one of the world's most battered cities is experiencing an astonishing revival. Hundreds of millions of dollars have poured into real estate and other businesses, exports of livestock and fruit have soared, and the government predicts economic growth of 6 percent this year.

AMISOM's secret? Its readiness to bleed. Though it does not disclose casualties, the number of AMISOM soldiers killed in Somalia is estimated at 1,000 to 3,000. That level of casualties would be "totally unacceptable in a U.N. setting," says Doss. But since Uganda, Ethiopia, Kenya and Djibouti have all been attacked by Al-Shabab, all of these countries are prepared to pay that price. The same self-interest helps explain why, since most peacekeeping missions are in Africa, that continent now provides half of all peacekeepers in the world (or 60 percent if you include AMISOM).

Skeptics will worry that China's sudden conversion to peacekeeping—especially if it's of the more aggressive AMISOM-style variety—is little more than an exercise in soft power in a region where it has rapidly become a major player. Humanitarians will likely be concerned about the possible erosion of peacekeeping's traditional neutrality. But returning the responsibility to protect Africa to Africans aligns with the mood of an Africa that is increasingly assertive and ever more tired of the U.N. After all, the new peacekeeping mission there can hardly do worse than the old one.

Under the Sea: Russia, China and American Control of the Waterways

By Simon Reich
The Conversation, November 11, 2015

In the summer of 2007, in a bizarre incident shown live on Russian television, scientists accompanied by a couple of senior politicians descended 4,300 meters to the floor of the Arctic Ocean in two Mir mini submarines. Divers then planted a Russian flag on the seabed, and Russia officially notified the United Nations that it was claiming the ridge as part of its sovereign territory.

In effect, the Chinese did the same kind of thing when they decided to start building islands in the South China Sea by dredging sand from the bottom of the ocean.

In both cases, the countries were creating new sovereign territory.

One implication of their declaration was that anyone traveling within the 12-mile limit defined by international law was traversing through their sovereign waters, and could only do so subject to their approval.

Indeed, the Chinese take their claim so seriously that last week it even threatened that it "is not frightened to fight a war with the US in the region" to protect its sovereignty.

So the question is: why do American policymakers care about seemingly insignificant tracts of land so far away from America's shores?

International Law and American Concerns

International law is pretty clear. You can't declare any territory submerged under the sea outside the conventional 12-mile limit as your own, although you may have some privileges in the waters that lie immediately beyond it. You certainly can't build up some land to above the waterline, thus creating an island, and call it part of your own territory. And in neither case can you legitimately control access by other vessels. Indeed, no international commission has upheld the Russian or Chinese claims. But that hasn't stopped either the Chinese or the Russians from trying.

Americans, however, are pretty emphatic when it comes to denying such claims have any legitimacy.

In the Russian case, American policymakers were understandably caught off guard and bemused by this strange symbolic act.

But, at the same time, American policymakers have a right to be worried. Climate change could vastly increase sea traffic through the Arctic Ocean. And the future implications of Russian control of these sea-lanes have lots of potential downsides, given recent friction over Ukraine and Syria.

In the Chinese case, Americans were caught off guard and bemused when they shouldn't have been.

The Chinese have been making claims for a long time about their sovereignty over huge portions of both the East and South China Sea. But in this case, Americans are worried about what China's control of these waterways might do now to these commercial shipping lanes. Every year an estimated 50% of the world's total of commercial trade plus oil passes through the area.

Global Trade and American National Security

The question of why we do care isn't as obvious as it may seem.

America's policymakers declare that the maintenance of global trade and commerce is in its national security interests. So America needs to keep these shipping lanes open to what they call "freedom of navigation."

What that means is that they can send an Aegis class destroyer (so this was a powerful ship, not the equivalent of a coast guards vessel) and sail it past the Subi Reef (think of an island so small it would drive you mad if it was deserted and you had to live on it alone). It's the equivalent of a drive-by—just to send a message.

Then you put the US secretary of defense on an aircraft carrier, the *USS Roosevelt*, and do it again—just to ensure that both the Chinese and America's important regional allies understood the message:. "This isn't your territory—and our mighty navy is not about to allow you to push us out."

You might understandably assume that the Chinese, with their huge volume of exports, would also want to maintain open seas. And that the Russians would want to ship oil and gas to keep their economy afloat by water. So there is nothing to worry about.

But that's where more modest concerns about global trade are replaced by those about deeper, hardcore national security interests. For Americans there is a difference between "our" open seas and "their" open seas.

Freedom of Navigation and American Doctrine

A central element of American national security doctrine is the notion of "Freedom of Navigation" or FON.

In effect, we (Americans) assert our right to sail where we want, when we need to. Behind that, however, is the deeply embedded concept of "control of the commons."

Military historian Alfred Thayer Mahan popularized this idea over 130 years ago. He stressed the importance of America's navy in ensuring the free flow of international trade. The seas were his "commons."

Mahan argued that the British Empire was able to retain its commercial and military advantage by ensuring its ships could go anywhere. And that it could deny anyone else from doing so, if needed, in times of war. The overriding lesson is that wars are not won on the land. They are won on the sea by denying your adversary access to resources.

Today, Mahan's work remains a core element of America's military doctrine. It is taught to America's naval officers at their major training academy where he himself once worked and where his work is still regarded as having biblical significance. But it no longer is just applied to commercial trade. It now is applied to the access of its military in all kinds of commons—in the air, on the sea, in space and even in cyberspace.

> **International law is pretty clear. You can't declare any territory submerged under the sea outside the conventional 12-mile limit as your own, although you may have some privileges in the waters that lie immediately beyond it.**

So American policy-makers become frustrated when they believe Chinese hackers spy on the US or they build islands because it demonstrates that the US can't "control" that commons.

The answering message is clear. As Ash Carter, the US Secretary of Defense, said in a speech about Russia last week "At sea, in the air, in space and in cyberspace, Russian actors have engaged in challenging activities." Carter went on to make it clear that the US wouldn't tolerate Russian efforts to control those domains. Responding to Chinese threats, he also clearly implied in the same speech that China's continued activities could indeed lead to conflict.

The Importance of Chokepoints

But the sea remains the priority when it comes to controlling the commons.

And Chinese sovereignty over the South China Sea offers the prospect that a key trading route located in a narrow strip of water between land masses either side, what they call a chokepoint could be closed by the Chinese, in the future, if not today.

The Malacca Strait on the Western end of the South China Sea is one chokepoint—the immediate object of the US' concern last week. The Strait of Hormuz in the Persian Gulf, where much of the world's oil passes through, is another. And, at least according to the US Congressional Research Service, the Arctic Ocean, where the Russian planted their flag, could become another.

So this leaves the Americans with an abiding dilemma.

They are saddled with a grand military doctrine built on the principle of keeping the globe's key access points freely accessible to the US. The barely audible counterpart is that it should maintain a capacity to deny that access to any potential adversary in case of war. The doctrine, however, in practice can itself engender conflict—as we saw with the Chinese.

America may have a much bigger military capacity and even newer technologies that allow it to fight conventional wars. But defending the open seaways is expensive and often counterproductive. The Chinese, for example, are the world's largest importer of fossil fuels and China is far more dependent on foreign oil than the newly fossil fuel independent United States.

So critics ask why the US is defending the Persian Gulf when the Chinese are the prime beneficiaries?

The answer, it appears, has far more to do with military strategy than with global commerce.

Bibliography

"6 Facts About How Americans and Chinese See Each Other." *Pew Research*. Pew Research Project. Mar 30 2016. Web. 25 Apr 2016.

Ashton, Adam. "U.S. and Chinese Troops Connect in First-Ever Exchange at JBLM." *The News Tribune*. The McClatchy Company. Nov 20 2015. Web. 20 Apr 2016.

Balin, Zachary. "Balancing Cooperation and Competition in U.S.-China Relations." *Brookings*. Feb 19 2016. Web. 25 Apr 2016.

Barboza, David. "China Drafts Law to Boost Unions and End Abuse." *New York Times*. New York Times Company. Oct 13 2006. Web. 25 Apr 2016.

Blake, Andrew. "China Urges FBI to Strengthen Cybersecurity, Counterterrorism Cooperation with Beijing." *Washington Times*. The Washington Times, LLC. Mar 15 2016. Web. 20 Apr 2016.

Borger, Julian and Tom Phillips. "How China's Artificial Islands Led to Tension in the South China Sea." *The Guardian*. Guardian News and Media. Oct 27 2015. Web. 20 Apr 2016.

Branigan, Tania. "Ethnic Violence in China Leaves 140 Dead." *The Guardian*. Guardian News and Media. Jul 6 2009. Web. 26 Apr 2016.

Brownlee, Lisa. "China-based Cyber Attacks on US Military Are 'Advanced, Persistent and Ongoing': Report." *Forbes*. Forbes, Inc. Sep 17 2015. Web. 26 Apr 2016.

Callen, Tim. "Gross Domestic Product: An Economy's All." *IMF*. International Monetary Fund. Mar 28 2012. Web. 20 Apr 2016.

"China 2030: Building a Modern, Harmonious, and Creative Society." *World Bank*. International Bank for Reconstruction and Development. 2013. Web. 20 Apr 2016.

"China Economic Growth Slowest in 25 Years." *BBC News*. Jan 19 2016. Web. 20 Apr 2016.

"China Issues Report Attacking US Human Rights Record." *The Guardian*. Guardian News and Media. Jun 26 2015. Web. 25 Apr 2016.

"China's 8-7 National Poverty Reduction Program." *Worldbank*. The World Bank. Shanghai Poverty Conference. 2004. Web. 26 Apr 2016.

"China's Environmental Crisis." *CFR*. Council on Foreign Relations. Jan 18 2016. Web. 6 Apr 2016.

"Chronology of U.S.-China Relations, 1784–2000." *State*. U.S. Department of State. Office of the Historian. 2000. Web. 26 Apr 2016.

Chunying, Xin. "A Brief History of the Modern Human Rights Discourse in China." *Human Rights Dialogue*. Dec 4 1995. Web. 25 Apr 2016.

Conathan, Michael and Scott Moore. "Developing a Blue Economy in China and the United States." *American Progress*. Center for American Progress. May 2015. Pdf. 6 Apr 2016.

"Country Reports on Human Rights Practices for 2015." *State*. Bureau of Democracy, Human Rights and Labor. U.S. Department of State. 2015. Web. 26 Apr 2016.

Crawford, Jamie. "U.S. Protests after Chinese Military Jet Lands on South China Sea Island." *CNN*. Cable News Network. Apr 19 2016. Web. 20 Apr 2016.

Denyer, Simon. "China's War on Terror Becomes All-Out Attack on Islam in Xinjiang." *The Washington Post*. Nash Holdings. Sep 19 2014. Web. 20 Apr 2016.

Esposito, Mark and Terence Tse. "China Is Expanding Its Economic Influence in Africa. What Is Africa Getting Out of It?" *Slate*. Slate Group. Nov 24 2015. Web. 20 Apr 2016.

"FACT SHEET: President Xi Jinping's State Visit to the United States." *Whitehouse*. Office of the Press Secretary. Sep 25 2015. Web. 6 Apr 2016.

"FACT SHEET: U.S.-China Economic Relations." *Whitehouse*. Office of the Press Secretary. Sep 25 2015. Web. 20 Apr 2016.

"Freedom on the Net 2015." *Freedom House*. Freedom House. 2015. Web. 25 Apr 2016.

Freeman, Charles III. "U.S.-China Relations: Challenges for the 114th Congress." *NBR*. National Bureau of Asian Research. 2014. Web. 26 Apr 2016.

French, Howard W. "China's Dangerous Game." *The Atlantic*. Atlantic Monthly Group. Nov 2014. Web. 20 Apr 2016.

Gillespie, Patrick. "China Contagion: How it Ripples Around the World." *CNN Money*. Cable News Network. Aug 26 2015. Web. 20 Apr 2016.

Hunt, Katie. "China to Narrow Gap with U.S. by Increasing Military Spending." *CNN*. Cable News Network. Mar 5 2015. Web. 26 Apr 2016.

Johnson, William. "Everything You Need to Know About the South China Sea Conflict—In Under Five Minutes." *Reuters*. Thompson Reuters. Jun 9 2015. Web. 6 Apr 2016.

"Joint Press Release of the Quadrilateral Coordination Group on Afghan Peace and Reconciliation." *State*. U.S. Department of State. Jan 11 2016. Web. 20 Apr 2016.

Kissinger, Henry A. "The Future of U.S.-Chinese Relations." *Foreign Affairs*. The Council on Foreign Relations. Apr 2012. Web. 25 Apr 2016.

"Mass Crackdown on Chinese Lawyers and Defenders." *Hrichina*. Human Rights in China. Feb 5 2016. Web. 25 Apr 2016.

Monaghan, Angela. "China Surpasses US as World's Largest Trading Nation." *The Guardian*. Guardian News and Media. Jan 10 2014. Web. 20 Apr 2016.

Nuccitelli, Dana. "Fact Check: China Pledged Bigger Climate Action than the USA; Republican Leaders Wrong." *The Guardian*. Guardian News and Media Limited. Nov 14 2014. Web. 6 Apr 2016.

Page, Jeremy, Lee, Carol E., and Gordon Lubold. "China's President Pledges No Militarization in Disputed Islands." *The Wall Street Journal*. Dow Jones & Company. Sep 25. 2015. Web. 20 Apr 2016.

Rapoza, Kenneth. "Top 10 China Dependent Countries." *Forbes*. Forbes Inc. Nov 26 2015. Web. 26 Apr 2016.

Ruz, Camila. "Human Rights: What is China Accused Of?" *BBC News*. Oct 21 2015. Web. 24 Apr 2016.

Sedghi, Ami. "China v the US: How the Superpowers Compare." *The Guardian*. Guardian News and Media Limited. Jun 7 2013. Web. 3 Apr 2016.

Small, Andrew, Wei, Zhu, and Eric Hundman. "Is China a Credible Partner in Fighting Terror?" *Foreign Policy*. The FP Group. Nov 24, 2015. Web. 26 Apr 2016.

Tang, Didi. "China's 168 Million Migrants Workers Are Discovering Their Labor Rights." *Business Insider*. Apr 6 2015. Web. 25 Apr 2016.

Taylor, Lenore. "US and China Strike Deal on Carbon Cuts in Push for Global Climate Change Pact." *The Guardian*. Guardian News and Media. Nov 12 2014. Web. 26 Apr 2016.

"The East in Grey." *The Economist*. Economist Newspaper Limited. Aug 10 2013. Web. 6 Apr 2016.

"The Indispensable Economy?" *The Economist*. The Economist Newspaper Limited. Oct 28 2010. Web. 25 Apr 2016.

"The United States and China to Extend Visas for Short-term Business Travelers, Tourists, and Students." *State*. U.S. Department of State. Nov 10 2014. Web. 20 Apr 2016.

"The U.S.—China Relationship." *PBS*. Frontline. WGBH Educational Foundation. 2001. Web. 25 Apr 2016.

"Tiger Chairs and Cell Bosses." *HRW*. Human Rights Watch. May 13 2015. Web. 25 Apr 2016.

"Tilton, Sarah. "Zhang Weiwei Talks About His New Think Tank, U.S.-China Relations and Why He Loves Bhutan." *Forbes*. Forbes Inc. Oct 30 2015. Web. 26 Apr 2016.

"U.S.-China 21: The Future of U.S.-China Relations Under Xi Jinping." *Asiasociety*. Asia Society Policy Institute. 2016. Web. 25 Apr 2016.

"U.S.-China Climate Change Working Group Fact Sheet." *U.S. Department of State*. Office of the Spokesperson. Jul 10 2013. Web. 4 Apr 2016.

"U.S.-China Joint Presidential Statement on Climate Change." *Whitehouse*. Office of the Press Secretary. Sep 25 2015. Web. 6 Apr 2016.

"U.S.-China Relations Since 1949." *Columbia University*. Columbia University. Asia for Educators. 2009. Web. 25 Apr 2016.

Velez-Hagan, Justin. *The Common Sense Behind Basic Economics: A Guide for Budding Economists*. New York: Lexington Books, 2015. Pg 111.

Webster, Graham. "2015: The Year US-China Relations Went Public." *The Diplomat*. Trans-Asia, Inc. Dec 23 2015. Web. 20 Apr 2016.

"Why Is There Tension Between China and the Uighurs?" *BBC News*. Sep 26 2014. Web. 20 Apr 2016.

Wike, Richard and Bridget Parker. "Corruption, Pollution, Inequality Are Top Concerns in China." *Pew Global*. Pew Research Center. Sep 24 2015. Web. 25 Apr 2016.

Wong, Edward. "China Urging Afghanistant to Restart Peace Talks With Taliban." *New York Times*. New York Times Company. Jan 27 2016. Web. 20 Apr 2016.

Wong, Edward. "U.S. Case Offers Glimpse Into China's Hacker Army." *New York Times*. New York Times Company. May 22 2014. Web. 20 Apr 2016.

"World Economic Outlook (WEO) Update." *IMF*. International Monetary Fund. Jan 2016. Pdf. 20 Apr 2016.

"World Report 2015: United States." *HRW*. Human Rights Watch. 2015. Web. 25 Apr 2016.

Yun, Sun. "China's Foreign Aid Reform and Implications for Africa." *Brookings*. Brooking Institution. Africa in Focus. Jul 1 2015. Web. 25 Apr 2016.

Zhang Hongzhou. "China's Evolving Fishing Industry: Implications for Regional and Global maritime Security." *RSIS*. S. Rajaratnam School of International Studies Singapore. Aug 16 2012. Web. 6 Apr 2016.

Zimmerman, James. "Stalled Chinese Reforms, Stalled Chinese Economy." *Wall Street Journal*. Dow Jones & Company. Apr 13 2016. Web. 20 Apr 2016.

Websites

Brookings Institution

www.brookings.edu

The Brookings Institution is a Washington, D.C. think tank that conducts research on the social sciences, economics, governance, foreign policy, and economic development. Brookings produces research that is often used by journalists, researchers, and policymakers on key U.S. issues. The Center has an international center in Beijing, China and frequently produces studies and public opinion polls on U.S.-China issues.

Carnegie-Tsinghua Center for Global Policy in Beijing

Carnegietsinghua.org

The Carnegie-Tsinghua Center for Global Policy in Beijing is an academic organization focused on China's foreign policy and domestic policy issues. Experts from a variety of fields contribute to the organization's articles and participate in foreign relations issues between China and the United States.

China Labor Watch

Chinalaborwatch.org

China Labor Watch is an independent, nonprofit organization that reports on labor and worker's rights issues in China. Articles published through the organization's website discuss the activities of foreign corporations in China and legislation on worker's rights issues.

China Labour Bulletin

www.clb.org.hk

China Labour Bulletin is a worker's rights organization that supports legislation and grassroots movements promoting collective bargaining rights, trade union organization, and labor rights organization. The CLB is allied with the All-China Federation of Trade Unions.

China Research Center

www.chinacenter.net

The China Research Center is a U.S.-based academic and research organization founded in 2001 promoting an understanding of Chinese culture and history. The center works with academic and governmental organization to support student exchanges between the two countries and joint academic and institutional collaborations between academics and experts representing the two nations and hosts an annual speaker series.

China-United States Exchange Foundation

www.chinafocus.com/2022/

The China-United States Exchange Foundation hosts meetings between Chinese legislators, academics, and economic leaders towards the goal of building stronger economic ties between the two nations. The foundation's U.S.-China 2022 program is a comprehensive study on the current and potential future of U.S.-Chinese economic relations through 2022.

Council on Foreign Relations

www.cfr.org

The Council on Foreign Relations is an independent think tank and publisher focused on U.S. foreign relations. The organization has published blogs, articles, books, and reports on diplomacy and foreign relations issues and also supports roundtable discussions with academic and legislative experts.

The Diplomat

thediplomat.com

The Diplomat magazine is an online-only publication focused on political and foreign relations developments in the Asia-Pacific region. The magazine covers Chinese politics, military development, and business initiatives in the Asia-Pacific region.

Ministry of Foreign Affairs of the People's Republic of China

www.fmprc.gov.cn

China's Ministry of Foreign Affairs outlines the nation's efforts in diplomacy, foreign relations, and foreign investment projects. Press releases from the PRC government highlight the nation's internal perspective on foreign relations issues.

National Bureau of Asian Research

www.nbr.org/research

The National Bureau of Asian Research is a nonprofit research organization based in Seattle, Washington that provides research and information to guide U.S. policy with regard to Asia. The organization has conducted in-depth studies on U.S.-Chinese political strategy and economic cooperation.

National Committee on U.S.-China Relations

www.ncuscr.org

The National Committee on U.S.-China Relations is a nonprofit organization founded in 1966 that seeks to further diplomatic contact between the United States and China. The Committee hosts speakers, educational programs, and maintains a collection of records of past diplomatic contact between U.S. and Chinese leaders.

Pew Research Center

www.pewresearch.org

The Pew Research Center is a think tank based in Washington, D.C. that conducts studies and public opinion polls on a variety of social and political issues. The Pew Research archive contains a variety of studies on pressing issues in Chinese society, with a focus on China's economic and social development and the evolution of U.S.-Chinese relations.

United States Department of State

www.state.gov

The United States Department of State (DOS) is the branch of the U.S. federal government charged with issues surrounding international relations and foreign contact. The DOS contains an archive of press releases describing past and current diplomatic programs involving U.S. and Chinese leaders.

The U.S.-China Perception Monitor

www.uscnpm.org

The Carter Center is a nonprofit public policy center founded by former President Jimmy Carter that seeks to address poverty, oppression, and human rights issues internationally. The Center launched the U.S.-China Perception Monitor in 2013 with the goal of exploring cultural and social misconceptions between China and the United States towards helping decision makers and leaders to make decisions regarding policy. The center collects articles discussing various aspects, past and present, of the U.S.-China relationship.

The White House

www.whitehouse.gov

The White House is the official website for the executive administration of the United States. The website contains an archive of statements and releases on presidential and executive office functions, meetings with foreign dignitaries, and legislative initiatives.

Wilson Center Kissinger Institute on China and the United States

www.wilsoncenter.org

The Kissinger Institute on China and the United States (KICUS) is a branch of the Wilson Center focused on collecting news and information related to U.S.-China relations to inform public discourse and to guide public policy developments. The institute produces a monthly newsletter with links to web and print articles and press releases from related governmental and research organizations.

Index